I Understood

a novel

I Understood

a novel

Ahmed A.S.

Arnold Heinemann

First Published, 1985

Publlished by Gulab Vazirani for Arnold Heinemann Publishers
(I) Pvt., AB/9 Safdarjang Enclave, New Delhi-110029 and
Printed at Man-Hari Printers New Delhi.

1

It was in the middle of July, nearing midday at the centre of Muttrah as I sat under a wooden shed to await my turn to enter the clinic. It was hot. The few pedestrians who ventured out of doors to carry out their errands in the searing heat walked briskly with bowed heads, bent on completing their chores as quickly as possible in order to return to the protection of the shade. When the woman who sat opposite to me suddenly burst out into shrill laughter, no one paid any attention to her. One passer-by did glance at our direction. He did so only instinctively, however, and continued on his way at the same rapid pace. He was, like everybody else, too uncomfortable in the heat to indulge his curiosity.

After running its course, the woman's mirth ceased as abruptly as it had begun. She gazed at the ground directly in front of her. She seemed totally oblivious of her surroundings. A secretive smile stirred her lips uncertainly as she deliberated with herself in wry humour. A few moments later, with startling abruptness she commenced her mysterious laughter. I thought I detected a hint of desperation in her anguished mirth; a hidden but unmistakable plea for recognition of her plight. Or, at least, understanding and sympathy from someone.

A fleeting glance from a pedestrian, made on impulse, was all the attention the anguished cry of the suffering woman attracted.

I gazed impassively at the woman for a second or two, and then uncertainly moved my gaze to the empty horizon. At first, it appeared natural to me that the unknown woman should have acted the way she did. It was only later, after my slow, erratic intellect had toyed with and dimly examined the situation that I became aware of the oddity of her behaviour. Unlike other spectators, however, (there were other patients seated nearby, together with their escorts) I understood only too well the aberration which produced the curious spectacle.

Presently, a plump nurse opened the door of the clinic and summoned the woman. She rose and followed the nurse inside. As I sat idly, awaiting for my summons an old, white-bearded man approached. Awkwardly, he inquired whether the adjacent clinic was the one for mental cases. I replied that it was. Reassured by my measured response, he explained that he had a nephew who needed such care. He described briefly the antics of his sick nephew. I clucked my sympathies and bade him await his turn.

The woman came out of the clinic as I was summoned by the same nurse to go in. As the former passed close to me I greeted her. Her eyes lit up with lively interest as she returned my greeting. She inquired after my health, to which I responded falsely, but properly, to the effect that all was well. Propriety required that the conversation be prolonged somewhat, since we hadn't even been introduced to each other. I did not take the initiative to prolong the awkward intercourse, although I very much desired to do so. She didn't make any effort to continue the discourse either, so clumsily, we parted. I thought her eyes were a shade too bright, the only suspect feature in an otherwise wholesome and stable countenance.

My gaze, erratic and expressionless, followed the woman as she walked away to mingle with the sweating mass of humanity milling around the central market. She would walk directly to her house, I thought. She wouldn't visit any one, even if she passed by a relative's house in whose midst a road accident had untimely taken away the life of a loved one. On reaching home, she would sit on a rug made of palm-tree leaves and gaze in front of her, an uncertain smile on her lips, disbelief in her eyes. She wouldn't do any work. She would eat a meal when it was brought to her. Afterwards, due to the force of habit, she would rise to wash her hands. Visitors would come to inquire after her health. Mostly old women of her age, they would chatter and gossip and would endeavour to draw her into their confidence. She would listen politely to their discourse, but without enthusiasm or interest. Gradually, the effort needed to do justice to her guests would prove too much for her. She would detach herself and lapse into silence. She would abruptly emit a curiously humorous, faintly hysterical, tormented shriek of mirth.

So clear were the conflicting emotions conveyed that I could easily make out the various sensations contained in the outburst.

I wondered why the woman went to the trouble of finding a psychiatrist. To start with, she couldn't communicate with the man since she knew neither English nor Arabic. She could speak only Swahili, her mother-tongue. She couldn't explain what was the matter with her even if there had been no language barrier: her predicament defied explanations. Furthermore, if she had believed that there was the remotest chance of a cure, or relief, she would have turned to religious scholars for the kind of help she understood and believed in. I knew that she knew there was no possible treatment of any kind, nor relief through any medication. I knew that she knew her case was hopeless. The only possible cure was to wipe her memory clean: she wouldn't accept that. After all, the torments and agony, the pain and regrets were all she had as evidence that she had lived.....

The nurse hurried me impatiently. Giggling idiotically, I walked, zombie-like, into the clinic.

It was much later that the vague feeling that the hapless woman had aroused in my subconscious crystallized into conscious thought. Our chance encounter made for yet another coincidence in a sequence of curious coincidences that made a mockery of any rational laws of probability. I believed that I had no right to stretch logic so thin simply because I had no alternative explanation. So many coincidences could not be logical, I maintained emphatically. Yet they kept happening, nevertheless

She was barely ten. She was soot-black and pretty. Her eyes were large and clear, her teeth sparkling white and even. She wore a black length of cotton cloth around her little waist, and covered her back and chest with an additional piece of the same material. She carried a small bundle in her arms which she handled carefully. She hugged it and occasionally kissed the pale brown skin underneath several layers of wrappings. She loved the infant and was proud that it had been entrusted to her care.

A ten-years old maid, wearing a black cloath around her waist and chest, carrying in her arms an infant covered in many layers of wrappings.

The Maid, straightening the baby's wrappings trips, loses her balance and falls the infant onto mud-baked floor.

She was straightening the baby's wrappings, which had become entangled with her own when she slipped, lost her balance and dropped the precious bundle on to the hard, mud-baked floor. The baby shrieked. The little maid, frightened out of her wits, screamed in fear. The infant's mother rushed out to investigate. With a cry she fell to her knees and retrieved the baby. She examined it closely but, finding no trace of physical injury, thanked God as, she hugged and pressed the little bundle close to her heart.

She could not know of the fright and fear hidden within the delicate membranes of the infant's little brain, nor could she guess that the seed of horror had been planted, to be nourished and grow even as the baby nurtured and grew.

The beast was conceived. Like the baby, it would grow with time.

I came during the hard times. The year before my birth, my father had invested the remainder of his inherited wealth on a sesame plantation, following the success story of his friend who had doubled his fortune on a sesame field the previous rainy season. Unfortunately for my father, however, the rains did not come this time. The young shoots that made it out of the dry earthbed wilted in the heat and died. The few hardy ones that reached maturity made for a meagre harvest that barely covered the cost of labour. From then onwards, it was downhill for us.

My early years were unhappy ones. I remember the numerous visits to the hospital and the chubby face of the matronly lady-doctor more than my life at home. After more than a year of hospital treatment which brought no results, my father grew impatient and decided to call on the services of the local medicine-man. I remember well the day I tagged behind my father, holding his hand, to a rendezvous with the native doctor a short distance from home. We walked silently until we arrived at a cross-path to find the bearded doctor waiting for us. No greetings were exchanged. The bearded man pulled me from my father's grasp, and the two men then undressed me. My father held me firmly as the other man pierced my tender stomach with red-hot iron bars I had seen him preparing. I shrieked and writhed in pain. Thereafter, my visits to the hospital became less frequent.

Having lost his inheritance on the misguided plantation venture, my father's assets now consisted of a few rolls of cloth, strings of shiny beads, a bag of salt and another of ground corn-seeds. These constituted the basic requirements of the villagers. The men bought measurements of cloth which they wore around their bodies, with the opposite ends tied in a knot on one shoulder. The women wrapped the material around their waists. They also covered the upper parts with an additional piece of cloth to allow for female decency as well as ease of movement, and wore strings of colourful beads around the waist and neck.

My father's shop sold little. The villagers had had a poor harvest of corn due to the lack of rain. They had no extra corn to sell to my father, who would have had it ground in a machine owned by another shopkeeper for a small fee, and then resold it to the villagers at a considerably inflated price.

My maternal grandparents lived in relative comfort in Zanzibar. They owned sizeable clove plantations. My mother would travel to Zanzibar whenever she was heavy with child, to deliver the new-born near her parents. Gamal, the third elder brother, remained in Zanzibar and attended school there. He came to the mainland only occasionally, during the school holidays, to visit us. My own birth took place in our home village due to the disastrous financial loss caused by the investment mishap.

My father could not raise the money for the journey, and grandmother's offer to pay for the trip arrived too late.

I was about four when Gamal paid us a visit. He was then only about twelve, but I thought he was so much older. He was very handsome. I remember him most for the many times he changed his clothes. I would sit for hours, crosslegged, and stare at him as he changed from one trouser to another, trying them for size. He was so different from me I could not conceive the fact that he was a relation. I was dirty, shabbily-clad and weak. He was sparkling, robust and handsomely attired. In bafflement I tried to fathom the meaning of his relationship to me without success. I wondered from which magic land he had sprung.

My simple four-year-old mind could not untangle the puzzle. It registered only perplexity. It also registered the firm impression that I was poverty-stricken and dirty; and that somewhere, far away, there existed a magic land from which a handsome, imposing and wealthy relation had appeared.

The second monster was hatched. Like the first, it would nurture and grow with time.

Meanwhile I, too, grew up.

2

At the age of five I was enrolled in two schools simultaneously. In one, which I attended in the mornings, I studied religious lessons. Along with some one dozen other children, we were provided with small black-boards which we smeared with a mixture of soot and charcoal. We then wrote lessons on the charcoal-coated surface using short, pointed sticks. Our teacher showed us how to extract the juice from small legume plants which we used as ink. We would sit cross-legged on rugs made of sisal fibre in an open space of our teacher's home, and recite the religious verses. The reading went on for as long as the teacher was in attendance. As soon as he disappeared into the house, or left on his bicycle on an errand for his family, the reading ceased. We would then gossip or while away the time in some less strenuous pursuit. Sometimes the teacher caught us idling and the whipping would start. Later on, in his absence, we would hold council and discuss ways and means of exacting revenge. Suggestions ranged from hiding scorpions in his old sofa-seat to ganging up on him in the bush with our own whips. We never acted on our resolutions, however. Amongst other reasons, we knew that our parents were solidly behind the teacher.

Some months later, a new teacher was brought from another village to replace the incumbent. From the gossip some of the older children had overheard, we surmised that the latter had been dismissed because he was not strict enough with the little scholars. This of course meant that

the parents had concluded that he was not ready enough
to use the whip, hence our poor progress in mastering the
verses. The point was brought home to us unerringly the
morning following the new teacher's arrival. We reported
for class earlier than usual; partly as a mark of respect for
our new teacher. Primarily, however, it was on account of
our anxiety to measure him and, consequently, to assess
the chances for our future survival. He was older than our
former teacher, and decidedly sterner. He was an early
riser, too. We found him examining closely a bundle of
thick, newly-cut branches from a tamarind tree. The same
tree, I guessed, that grew near the foot-path midway from
my home to the school. He was so absorbed in the task he
seemed not to notice our arrival. We crouched near him
and stared in morbid fascination at the bundle of green
branches, some of which had leaves and little twigs still
attached to them. He picked one branch, examined it
closely, caressed it with the palm of his hand, and then
bent it in a full circle so that the two ends met. We
remembered our manners suddenly and greeted our new
teacher. Swoosh, the whip pierced the air noisily as he let
go of one end and it straightened to its original length.

At the other school, which I attended in the
afternoons, both the lessons and the style of initiation were
different. The teachers—two males and two females
respectively—taught us the English alphabet and
handwriting. There was no whipping, although we were
given such chores as cleaning and running errands for the
male teachers. We were also taught handiwork. This
consisted of peeling the outer skin out of sisal leaves to
expose the white strands of fibre underneath. We would
place the leaves on the side of our soles and, using a sharp

stone, rip the chaff away by pulling the leaves from under the stone. We used the fibre thus obtained for making brushes and brooms for the cleaning chores.

The female teachers taught the beginners' class, to which I belonged. One was slim, shy and pretty. Her eyes, expressive and intelligent, had a frightened look in them- rather like a bird. She was modest and very feminine. Her name was Ngima, Her colleague was the very opposite of her. Dawa was plain, fattish and immodest. Once, early in the afternoon, Dawa reproached the entire school for lack of punctuality. As we stood on roll-call she resolved mischievously to punish the lot of us. She inserted her hand inside my over-sized khaki shorts and pinched me lightly near the groin. She did the same to all the students, with the enthusiastic approval of the male teachers and the embarrassed stare of her female colleague. No one was really punished. Some of the older boys squealed delightedly.

Although I was years from puberty, my sexual drive was already substantial. I fell in love with the chocolate-coloured Ngima the first day I set eyes on her. Foolishly, I confided my feelings to a rascally little brat who could not keep the secret to himself. We were strolling in the woods. It was hot and humid and we were exhausted. We fell under a shade of a tree to take rest.

I felt profound waves of erotic sensations cascading all over my body. I let on to my little companion my feelings of attraction for our teacher. I described, in minute detail, the things I should do to her if and when I had my way with her. The following day, the whole school buzzed with the news. The little boys stared at me in perplexed fascination. The elder ones jeered at me for my folly. I felt uncomfortable and I was deeply embarrassed. I was also charged with apprehension lest the teacher, or her husband hear of it. (Ngima was married to the headmaster. Her husband taught only the morning classes, I discovered later) I blushed furiously whenever I caught her glance; and I avoided her whenever I could. I thought that she avoided me, too. Once, when running an errand for her husband unawares, I knocked at the door of her little white-painted house. She opened the door suddenly and fixed me with a wide, surprised gaze. Startled, with waves of apprehension running all over my body, I barely managed to stammer, in a cracking voice, the headmaster's message. I thought the garbled communication did not make any sense, but she understood at once. Without a word she went in and got hold of a spanner which she handed to me silently. I grabbed the thing and then cycled away hurriedly. I thought she had herself been greatly apprehensive. She had also appeared more frightened and vulnerable than usual.

In the evenings, after school, we played at the market place. We would make faces and tease each other. I was always the victim. Sometimes, in the summer, we captured fire-flies which we then kept in bottles. At other times we simply stood at the deserted market-place and shouted obscenities into the night.

With the shop business at a near standstill, father embarked on a new business venture. He purchased a few goats on credit from the villagers, slaughtered them and then resold the meat at about double the whole-sale price.

But this enterprise, too, failed: the villagers did not own the money with which to buy the costly meat. Father then decided to move us to the town to pursue his fortunes. Within a year, however, still unsatisfied with the direction of his fortunes, he packed us onto the train and off we moved again. After a whole day's journey we reached a major town. But our journey was not at an end. We were transferred to another train and, after a long delay, we journeyed on westwards for another full day. Finally, we arrived at our destination. A truck carried us and our bulky luggage to a home that was a considerable improvement from the former mud-roofed lodgings.

The new town was famed for its riches. It had a gold mine. Father had reasoned that the natives there should have more money with which to purchase the black and white clothes and beads. On arrival, however, we discovered that the natives there did not cover themselves with lengths of cloth; nor did their women-folk adorn themselves with colourful beads. Besides, there were several big and modern shops which catered for the requirements of the townsfolk. Undaunted, father opened a sweet-meat shop, using funds borrowed from a relative. Thankfully, business picked up briskly, for a change.

I resumed my interrupted studies in an all-boys' school. I did very well, earning several end of year honours. I also did well in the dramatics club. Every year on graduation day, the town elders and students's parents were invited to watch theatrical performances based on old English classics and some local themes. Invariably, I played roles which allowed me to wear my best attire ordered from England—much to the chagrin of a youthful teacher who disliked my dressing in anything but the shabby school uniforms. Perpetually well-groomed and neatly attired himself, the young teacher loathed to see me tastefully dressed lest I outshine him in the presence of the girls in town.

During the summer holidays I travelled by train to visit my uncle, who lived near our old home village. His hamlet was much smaller. It consisted of three shops and some muddy structures scattered in the periphery, belonging to the tribal villagers. My uncle's homestead was a small shack constructed of muddy bricks and supported by tree trunks. One had to bend one's head to enter the house. There were two rooms, one of which was occupied by my uncle and his wife. The other, which was located in the small backyard near the kitchen, was sublet to a paying guest. It was the guest's room that interested me. The guest tenant was a tall, thin man who walked uncertainly and did everything with a meek irresolution. He was seldom in the house. He would come to be with his wife for a couple of days after a long absence. His wife was young, big-boned and tall. Looking at her, one got the feeling that there was no ounce of flesh where it didn't belong. She was a splendid chunk of womanhood. She was also childish and in obvious need of sexual fulfillment. Her name was Elina.

After lunch, Elina played with her younger companion. Mwita was a twelve-year old kid sister of my uncle's wife. They constructed baby dolls of clay and laughed childishly as they moulded disproportionately large sexual organs. They also bathed together, giggling and chiding each other all the time. Then they would lie on Elina's bed and manipulate each other. They kept the door ajar to allow for daylight to reach the window-less room. I would sit in the enclosed yard and spy on their activities.

One day early in the morning an old man came to the house. He covered his head with a much used white cloth and talked continuously and solemnly to Elina. The latter was in the kitchen preparing food. She was out of view of the old man, but the light enclosure of wood and mud allowed his sombre voice to penetrate inside clearly enough. The old man talked for a good part of the day. Elina did not respond, but it was obvious that she was respectfully attentive to the old man's exhortations. It was nearing mid-day when the old man finally completed his preaching and departed. Thereafter, Elina and her companion restrained themselves from making open exhibitions of eroticism. They continued with their sensuous games, but with a token effort at concealment. They carried on in the privacy of the toilet or, when in the room, they kept the door a few degrees less wide-open. As I sat in the middle of the yard, ostensibly to watch the birds—which my uncle's wife domesticated—but in fact to peep at the half-naked women, my uncle awkwardly admonished me not to show undue interest in the girls. Unbeknown to me, my excessive interest in them had used a domestic crisis. Elina's father had been called to restrain his daughter from making such displays. Her husband had noticed my attraction and had lodged strong complaints to my uncle.

My secret lust for Elina having been exposed, I could no longer while the time of day in the backyard watching the birds. I did not know what to do with myself. Then my uncle left on a day-long trip to the town; leaving his double-barrelled shotgun behind. I decided to go hunting.

I asked my uncle's muscular, odd-job helper to accompany me. The huge man, who possessed little good sense, was excited with the idea. I stole the gun from my uncle's room and handed it to the gargantuan servant to carry for me. I led the way into the turfy hinterland. The bearer, singing praises of my gunmanship, followed a few paces behind. He also pledged, in a sing-song voice, that he would carry the biggest game I shot. We wandered for hours in the hilly terrain, but for a small pack of fighting wild dogs, found no game. We returned late at night to find my uncle anxiously waiting for me. He fretted a little and then inquired, with sarcastic humour, where I had kept the kill. I told him that I hadn't fired a shot.

The following day Elina handed me a coin and requested me to buy a bonbon at the neighbour's shop for her. I told her to keep her coin and I would bring her the candy. I thought, as I walked to buy the globular piece of saccharine, that if a bonbon was Elina's idea of savouriness, she was one big sorrowful waste of sweetmeat.

3

Soon after, I returned home to resume my studies. I woke up early in the morning and pedalled my bicycle away, passing by the stiff Indian shop-keeper who wore his coat a few sizes too big. As he walked, he tapped one end of the garment, gently, several times with his shoulder blade to attune it with his figure. A few paces further on, however, the coat again fell askew at the other end. He then tapped it again with the other shoulder to balance it.

And thence, for the fifteen minutes of his walk, he tapped his coat alternately with his shoulder-blades to adjust it on him.

Near our home lived an ancient Indian gentleman who was married to an equally old native woman. The product of their union was a fair, cream-coloured girl of about my age. I chased the girl for nearly two years without success. Although she was as attracted to me as I was to her, we never made contact. I was so shy and uncertain I failed to make use of the many opportunities she presented to me for a romantic encounter. Finally we both grew bored of the affair and drifted apart. I tried my luck with other girls in town. I wrote love letters and distributed them to several Asian girls through their house-servants and paid couriers. None responded.

My eldest brother, Mabruk was away in Arabia. He left us when we were still in our home village. He wrote to us only occasionally, and the letters took months to reach us. The last letter we received from him contained money orders. These were to be used to purchase airline tickets for my travel to Cairo. Mabruk desired that as many as possible of his younger kin pursue further studies abroad. The previous year he had paid for Gamal's trip. I was to join the latter in Egypt.

It was the day previous to my train journey to the capital, and thence onward to Cairo, when I encountered a group of the prettiest girls in town. They were holding a conference with a native houseboy. The girls did the talking: they were wrapping up the deal they had struck with him, and were repeating the terms of the contract in clear language so there should be no misunderstanding. The place was to be at a go-down belonging to one of the

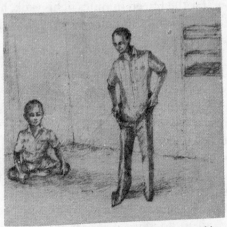

Four-year old boy, weak-looking, dirtily-clad in shabby shirt and shorts sitting cross-legged and staring at robust and handsome 14-year old relative trying exquisite dresses for size

A fair Sixteen-year old adolescent (Boy) crossing a small-town lane, meets a group of girls (Asian) talking with a bare-chested native houseboy (African) and is surprised by the discussion he overhears.

girl's father. The time was to be early evening. One girl, concerned that the servant (who did not own a watch) would miss the rendezvous on account of the time factor, used her hand to depict the appointed time in a clear, graphic description.

She raised her pretty hand to pinpoint the sun's position prior to sun-set, and then lowered it to level with the horizon. The houseboy nodded his head several times to reaffirm that he understood. He had seen me approaching and he knew that I was hearing the conversation. He became acutely embarrassed and wished that the girls would go away. The young ladies had seen me too. They, however, were unperturbed. They stressed that the deal cost two shillings. This was the main item of the contract and they made doubly certain that he understood before they finally took their leave, to the overwhelming relief of the bare-chested gentleman.

Two shillings. It was the amount charged by the wahayas (a well known prostitution-indulging tribe with members scattered all over the country). They charged two shillings for a short time session with the natives. Non-native locals were charged three shillings. The whores maintained that the latter belonged to a higher income group and should, therefore, pay them a fifty percent extra charge. Two shillings bought a cinema ticket in the back rows, or a pound of sweetmeat in my father's shop.

So much for my love letters and fashionable trousers. I recalled the trip I and two of my equally nit-witted friends had taken far into the hills in search of love charms. Someone had directed us to the abode of a villager said to posses the medicine that would charm the women right into our arms—for a price. We found the villager after a day long walk into the hilly countryside. For five shillings, he gave us a small bottle containing ground pawpaw roots mixed with sun-flower oil. Our instructions were to rub a woman's neck with the oil, and the charm should take care of the rest. Obviously, I thought, grinning as I walked. Besides which, I now came to realize, by the time I had a woman close enough to rub her neck with oil I wouldn't need love-attracting medicine anyway.

I might have known that hard cash held greater charm. It was nevertheless a startling revelation—and a rude blow to my self-esteem—to discover that what I couldn't achieve in two years of active pursuit could be had for two shillings—and then by a lowly house-servant. I, should have thought it an insult to offer money to the fair and seemingly virtuous young ladies belonging to the relatively well-do-do merchant community who, presumably, had enough money of their own, without the need to resort to cheap prostitution. Two shillings—for an experience I thought was magical and romantic.

It was a hard, if misplaced, lesson in realism fate would have been kinder to spare a young mind. I thought of postponing my journey to Cairo now that I had discovered a short cut to the satisfaction of my strong sexual urges. I realized, however, that I should need a better reason than this to persuade my parents to agree. Father was to accompany me to the capital to help with the travel arrangements.

That night I stole into the kitchen where the little maid who helped mother with the laundry slept. She was amenable to my advances. She feigned sleep as my persistent caresses weakened her with desire. I asked her if she was unwell; she nodded. Using my stiff little manhood, I examined her forehead and mango-like breasts for a feverish condition.

Early the following morning, father and I caught the train to the city. It was a long journey. We arrived the following day just before noon. The ticket collector at the station-platform remarked to us importantly that we had now arrived at the big city we kept hearing about. Father, always indulgent, feigned amazement and marvelled at the view-less horizon, to humour the man. Father had travelled to the capital innumerable times. In his youthful heydays, he had plowed the shores of Arabia, Africa and India forwards and backwards.

I caught the plane to Cairo a few days later, transiting Nairobi for a night-stop at the airline's cost. At the hotel, a young English girl kept following me unobtrusively. I had on a brightly-coloured nylon sweater which was presented to me the previous year by my brother Gamal. It was a lovely affair which fitted me well. With my tailored, well-fitting trousers, I knew I cut a striking figure. The girl was frankly admiring. I assumed that she was an aircraft stewardess as there were no English couples at the breakfast table earlier that day. Her interest in me was curiously disturbing. She seemed perfectly at ease to admire me and cared not at all that I knew it. Her eyes reflected innocence and frankness. She was neither shy nor flirtatious. She seemed to dare me to embarass her for her honest admiration.

Twenty years later, I still see the honest and innocent face of the admiring teen-ager, and wonder why I never even smiled at her as a gesture of my appreciation for her interest in me.

My life in Cairo was uneventful. I met my brother Gamal, who I thought was every bit the perfection of manhood I knew from childhood, although less awe-inspiring now that I was older. Together we visited the museum and toured the pyramids. We also contacted Government offices in connection with my scholarship.

I did little studying. For several reasons, but mainly financial, I felt discouraged from making serious attempts to pursue academic goals. My scholarship entitled me to bed and board, plus a five pound monthly allowance as pocket money. I disposed of the five pounds the same day I pocketted them, and spent the remainder of the month penniless. I made no provision for the bus fare, nor for a cake of soap with which to wash my clothes. Neither did I provide myself with a new pair of socks, or razor-blades. Occasionally Mabruk sent me a cheque. I used the money to purchase new clothes. The balance, if any, of my brother's hard-earned money I spent in a night club; or at the riverside boats where, for a few pounds, I had a few minutes of sexual indulgence. The sessions were less than **satisfactory, however.** I consumed a lot of booze to boost my courage prior to the engagements. Consequently, orgasm took long in coming. The pimp would grow impatient with the delay: he would shout and kick my legs to hurry me to finish off. Often I got off the whore before reaching orgasm. The few times that I did ejaculate, the hurrying and the beatings made whatever pleasure I derived from the experience hardly worth the trouble.

Mabruk came to Cairo to pay me a visit. I did not recognize him. Seeing that I could not place him, he introduced himself, whereupon I embraced him warmly. He discovered that I was not attending any school. I explained to him the financial problems I was facing, and he enrolled me in a private boarding school. Here I had no financial worries. Nevertheless, my education was erratic: the boarding and tuition in the private school proved too expensive for my brother's resources. Within a year I stopped boarding in the school and lodged in private quarters. The old problems recurred: I spent all the money I received from my brother within a few days and stayed penniless until the next cheque arrived. The subsequent remittance would take anything from a few weeks to several months. I barely managed to eat and survive. I would borrow some money from the landlord, change lodgings and borrow some more from the new landlord. When the cheque came, I paid the old debts and repeated the trick.

There were some dark moments. I once became a virtual prisoner in my quarters for several days. I had ordered some food, on credit, from a nearby restaurant. I had also purchased, again on credit, some groceries from a supermarket across the street; and I had borrowed hard cash from a neighbour who lived opposite my lodgings. I then discovered that whichever lane I took on my way out, I should encounter an enraged creditor who could not be put off any longer. So I closed myself in my quarters and waited for the cheque to arrive. The cheque did not come. I was starving and did not know what to do. Fortunately, I remembered one acquaintance from whom I hadn't borrowed any money. I stole out in the dead of the night and walked several miles to borrow money from the new source. Luckily, I found the gentleman, who, seeing the shape I was in, agreed to lend me a few pounds.

I used the money to buy groceries, including a sackful of rice. I had been close to starvation and was now careful to ensure that I had enough food to last me for as long as it took for the next remittance to arrive. After I had paid the taxi fare and settled in my single-room apartment, I had no money left but for some loose change. I decided to cook myself a good meal. I discovered that the gas had run out. I did not possess the half-pound with which to buy fresh gas, nor did I know anyone from whom I could borrow the money: I owed money to everyone I knew.

I felt beaten and came close to tears. Then I remembered Sami, a one-time friend and room-mate. Sami went to the same school as I, but he attended a higher class. For reasons somewhat similar to mine, he seldom appeared at school, except occasionally in the evenings to take a dip at the swimming pool. Lately, Sami and I had parted ways: I had discovered that he was a small time, cunning thief. He got me to borrow valuable items and things from students, which he sold secretly and pocketted the money. I would return to our room to find a chaotic, but stage-managed scene, with the landlord, neighbours and curious on-lookers gathered and getting drawn into the brawl. Everyone shouted at everybody else, with Sami accusing the lot of thievery. I would then realize, without being told, that the expensive recorder I had borrowed from a wealthy student, on Sami's gentle prodding, had been stolen. The large number of borrowed, and later stolen articles finally awoke me to the fact that I was being used as an unwitting accessory for a systematic swindle.

Despite our past quarrel, however, I carried the bag of
rice, together with other assorted groceries to Sami's place.
I was resigned to the fact that we should share the food. I
had no alternative. The following day I went to his room
for lunch, to find his large family settled all over the place.
Sami had told me that he was expecting his parents, but he
hadn't said how soon. I was hungry, but there was precious
little I could do about it. I could not ask for my groceries to
be returned to me: it would have been too embarrasing.
Besides I had once travelled with Sami to his home village,
where I had partaken of his family's substantial
hospitality. Once again I was at my wit's end. My only
course of action was to swallow my pride and become a
regular lunch-guest at Sami's place. The idea did not
appeal to me at all: I could not have Sami's family form the
impression that I depended on their son for my food, even
in the city. But I had no choice: I had to eat.

I became thoroughly disgusted with my life. I
experienced the anguish of total defeat. As my studies had
more or less come to an end, there was nothing to keep me
in Cairo. I sent an urgent appeal to Mabruk to take me
away.

4

I travelled to Saudi Arabia to look for work. I found a
job as a ticket salesman in a travel agency. My job entitled
me to reduced air transportation fare, and I made good use

of the privilege. But apart from the annual trips abroad, I had little to look forward to. I had no plans either for then or for the future. I was a loner, closed up and I never had a close friend. A perpetual sensation of pain below my tummy never seemed to leave me. Often I thought there was something the matter with me, but I never knew what it was. I seldom talked, and almost never listened. Whenever, I came near another person, or tried to converse, my heart would beat faster. It was as if I was being pulled by invisible strings away from contact with other people. I day-dreamed the days away and time passed.

I lived hurriedly, as though I had to catch up with something. But for the office work, which became more or less routine, I never did anything. Nevertheless, I lived in a perpetual hurry. I even hurried to go to bed, even though I didn't feel sleepy, Later on, I wrote stories to occupy my time.

In time, the surviving members of my family, was re-united in the land of our ancestry, following political upheavals in Zanzibar and a marked improvement in the fortunes of Oman.

In Salalah, I managed a small travel shop belonging to a trio of local entrepreneurs. I was relatively comfortable. I had a new car and lived in a modest company-provided apartment with modern amenities. Besides my job, I also acquired an equal share in a business enterprise consisting of two shops jointly owned with a partner. Khatib, my business partner, worked for the Government. A thin, insignificant-looking youth, he was markedly lacking in good looks. A non-smoking teetotaller, he had a pair of disproportionately long ears, a long, shapeless nose at the centre of a narrow face, slightly glazed brown eyes and tainted teeth. But what Khatib lacked in form was more than retrieved in substance: he was a solid, no nonsense realist. He lived with such a degree of propriety and exactitude that a gossipy old woman would have been hard put to find fault with him. He was married and lived in quiet precision in a Government-provided residential villa.

Amal, Khatib's wife, was as lovable and winsome a woman as any a man could desire. She was well-proportioned, affectionate and unpretentious. She had a dignified, quietly feminine bearing. She was also not unattractive. My shared business interests with her husband brought me ever closer to her. I was a regular visitor to their home and always partook of their gracious hospitality. She was one of only two women I ever felt close to in my life. In a round about way, through a third party—as was proper—Amal relayed to me the information that she had a relative of marriageable age and that further inquiries on her would be welcomed. It was proof of her affection and high regard for me that she had undertaken such an initiative on my behalf.

The other female I came to know well as a person—and not as a sex object—was Carol, a Swiss-born lady married to a local gentleman. Together with her husband Nadhim, we took evening walks together and occasionally drove to the military camp to watch a motion picture. The young but long-married couple had grown-up children, amongst whom was a sixteen-year old first-born daughter, Laura; who attended school in Switzerland. She had come to be with her parents for the summer vacation.

The struggling but happy couple desired strongly that I marry their adored young daughter. The rather wide age difference presented something of a dilemma to Nadhim who was uncertain of sanctioning a union for his daughter with someone so much older. He gave his consent, however. Like Carol, he hinted strongly that a marriage proposal would be welcomed. Young Miss Nadhim was in the flower of youth: the sweet age when the mind of an adolescent floated dreamily to womanhood as the body paused in anticipation. She, too, was agreeable to the proposition. She consented, however, out of deference to her family rather than from personal choice. As days passed without word from me, Carol became more insistent. She broached the subject of matrimony whenever we were together; and would display affectionate gestures towards her husband for my benefit. She would cuddle against him while I played table tennis with her daughter at the club. She talked at length on the subject as we were having a dinner treat with all her family in a restaurant; and pressed me to delay no further. As we walked out from a picture show at the army camp, she whispered that it needed but a word from me for the union with her daughter to take place. She was implying that the question of bridewealth was of no consequence of them. Poor Carol, she tried so hard.

The beginning of the academic year was approaching, and she had to reach a decision, together with her husband, on their children's schooling. Pressing financial commitments dictated the need for an early separation from their daughter in order to concentrate on the younger offspring. Laura understood her parent's difficulties. She was docile and did not protest at her mother's somewhat excessively forward attitude on the matter of her marriage.

I said nothing to Carol, one way or other, on the subject. Laura was frankly baffled. She could not understand the innocent expression on my face when our eyes met, as if I didn't understand what her mother was trying so hard to get across. She wondered, ironically, whether I was playing hard to get. After all, it should have been the other way round.

I had no word for Amal, either. She, too, expected an affirmative gesture from me, although she did not display the anxiety of Carol. As the business enterprises with her husband expanded, her interest in me naturally increased. She laughed more in my presence and allowed me to glimpse at intimate, but not unwarranted, moments with her husband she had not permitted earlier. Our business expanded to include a small boutique. Norla, an English lady whose expatriate husband worked for the Government, joined us in partnership. She stitched ladies' dresses which she sold in the shop together with the imported ones. Norla was dark, small in stature and very comely. She had close-cropped, copper-coloured hair which fell on her forehead, complementing her facial make-up most attractively. She was soft-spoken and agreeable. I liked to keep company with her. I also liked to impress her with an exaggerated opinion of myself both as an accomplished man of the world as well as a successful businessman.

Despite the relative prosperity, I was not happy. I grew more disenchanted with myself as time passed. I had no problems, financial or otherwise, to speak of. Nevertheless, I grew so bored with the aimless routine that my life was becoming an unbearable misery. I started to drink heavily. I totally neglected my office work, which in any case had ceased to interest me long ago. I thought the job was lowly and unworthy of my attention. I despised the owners, too. A semi-literate lot, I thought they affronted my worth for daring to hire me to work for them. I reported at the office only to wait for closing time. I ignored the work pointedly and totally. For the six months prior to my resignation, I worked for only about ten minutes. For the duration of the six months but for those ten minutes, I didn't even make a pretence of working. I would chat with Norla or simply sit still and wait for the hours to pass.

For the ten minutes that I did work, I felt a peculiar, if vague, sensation of well-being and worthiness. But I ignored the feelings, the way I ignored Amal and her affections. The way I ignored Carol and the love she bestowed on me. The way I ignored sweet Laura and her promises. The way I ignored everything that constituted the essence of living. The beasts, fully grown now, could be contained no longer. I felt a definite sensation of something struggling to break free from inside my throat. I never knew what it was. I thought it was some kind of ingenuity or talent of some sort about to manifest itself.

Little did I guess that it was a pair of horrific monsters the like of which few humans have known. I was at a club belonging to expatriate workers when I overheard a conversation that was to lead to the show down with the demons in my head. Two foreigners who sat near me were discussing business. One of them, an executive of the firm, was a slight acquaintance with whom I sometimes exchanged pleasantries. He was relating to the other man about a business project he had arranged with a local trader, who had failed to meet his end of the bargain. The foreigner was now stuck with unfinished business. I had had a fair amount of drinks, and I felt light-headed. I also felt a strong urge to talk. More to satisfy the urge to converse than to seriously tackle the gigantic project, I interrupted their discussions with an offer to undertake the business, provided the terms were agreeable. To my astonishment, the offer was taken seriously. We discussed the business for over an hour and concluded with a more or less firm commitment on my part to undertake the project.

I was all excitement as I drove home, well past midnight. I kept telling myself that I was going to pull it off.

I discussed the project with my partner. Through him we found a financial backer who agreed to sponsor it and join us on equal partnership. We contacted the bank, which demanded a feasibility study. I prepared one and handed it to them. The funds were provided. It was that simple.

My annual vacation was due, coinciding with the exciting arrangements for the new project. I went on numerous hectic trips: I flew to Europe on business and thence to the Far East for pleasure. I interrupted my stay in the East to fly again to Europe to sort out export documents for the machinery, and then flew back to resume my vacation in the Far East. As I was in charge of a travel office, most of my travels were first class. It took a while for the wonder of it all to sink in. As soon as I tried I pulled off a tremendous business coup that would have done credit to a veteran businessman. I had practically become a jet-setter; a millionnaire in the making. I mingled with international businessmen, shared jokes with them and matched wits with the best of them. Why,

36

whatever had kept me dumb all my life? I marvelled more and more at the wonder of it. After all, all I had done was to interrupt other people's conversation in a bar and within a month there I was: at the centre of events. I looked at the edge of my table and saw the unused first class return tickets to Nairobi I had not utilized because I had not found time. It was real, all right; the long-awaited self-discovery had occurred. I had found the real me.

Suddenly, I saw a vision in my mind: I had established a great business empire. With the instant turnover from the business I purchased the rockets of Cape Canaveral and blasted off to the centre of the universe, where I met the ruler of the Cosmos seated on an armchair. I querulously tried to push him off, but he refused to budge. I pushed again, but once more failed to move him. I gave a tremendous third push. The old bearded gentleman vacated the seat with dignity this time, and I sat in his place.

The beasts had broken loose, and all hell with them. There appeared a minute chain made of tiny, organic beads which linked my surface awareness with the dark abyss of the subconscious. The beads were progressively enlarged: the biggest was nearest my consciousness, and the smallest was placed at the end, a part of which disappeared in the inner darkness.

5

I flew to Europe once again, taking Norla with me

A fair 31 year old Man sees vision of omnipotence (thoughts and imaginations fly to centre of Universe)

Thoughts make tortuous return journey from heavens, passes through mind of 31 year old man and four year old boy and reaches infant, and returns to 31 year old man and normalcy.

this time: the better to impress her with my august position in the business affairs of the world. On my return from the trip I accidentally met, in Muscat, an old acquaintance of many years. Adwan held a high position in the airline business. Although we had known each other for a long time, and had once shared accomodation in Saudi Arabia, we were not close. When we met we exchanged polite greetings. Sometimes we shared gossip. Adwan had never been anything but polite to me. I had no cause to hate or fear him. Nevertheless, I always felt an unconscious undercurrent of guilt and fear of him on account of the neglect and contempt I felt for my job. I feared that he could do considerable damage to my means of livelihood if he discovered that I neglected my job and sent word to my employers, who held him in high regards. I was in a state of overexcitement and dizzying feeling of freedom from the lifetime of inhibitions from which I believed I was now emancipated. I was walking to a hotel acress the street for a drink, passing near a pair of dirty, slime-coated garbage drums the municipality kept near our house, when I emancipated. I was walking to a hotel across the street for a conceivable reason, I felt an irresistable compulsion to humiliate him. Accordingly, I raised an issue out of thin air in the course of which I brought home to him, in no uncertain terms, that he was very low in my estimation; and furthermore, that he was arrogant and capricious. Startled, the dignified gentleman nevertheless kept his cool. Despite his astonishment at the vehemence of the unsolicited accusations, he kept the peace and apologized for any breach of faith he may have committed, citing the demands of his work as possible causes for his unintentional misconduct.

In Salalah, I resumed the untenable defamation of the good gentleman's forthright character to my heart's contentment. With the satisfaction of this singular compulsion, the smallest bead in the chain was swallowed into the darkness.

My employers became jittery on learning of my many travels abroad, and I tendered my resignation. In the event, I had an unfortunate and violent quarrel with the local proprietor. The man held me in high esteem and had bestowed much kindness on me. But I despised and scorned him simply because he did not measure up to my idea of an intelligent employer.

Soon after, an Indian girl I had met a few times in Muscat came to Salalah. It was a curious coincidence that she came alone and at that particular period in my life. Julie had something with her that attracted my abnormal erotic impulses like a powerful magnent. She was very attractive. She wore tight-fitting dresses which displayed her gorgeous body to full advantage. But it was the way she talked that captivated me. She spoke with her lips raised and alternatively curled backwards, rather like a monkey. It was a curious factor to attract a man's sexual interest, but the affectation suited her most alluringly. I fell under a near-hypnotic spell as I watched her mouth constructing words.

Julie came to visit me in the shop and I invited her for lunch. As we were having our meals in the town's only modern cafeteria, she chatted non-stop throughout the meal. I listened to her interestedly and watched her pouting lips with rapidly rising excitement. She talked of her recent love affair; of how she had fallen madly in love with one man, but the depth of feeling wasn't mutual. The man, who had come to Salalah to work—and hence her journey to Salalah to be near him—had refused to marry her. (Julie was already married. Her husband, a young and presentable fellow Indian, worked for my brother at Muscat). So profound were her feelings for this man that she had undertaken a fake but dangerous suicide attempt in a bid to soften his heart enough to marry her—to no avail. She showed me the ugly marks under her armpits where she had slashed herself with a blade. Her feelings appeared genuine and I could not help but feel sympathy for her. It suddenly dawned on me that it was the first time in my life I had ever listened to anyone for so long. It was also the first time I had sympathised with anyone. It was a strange, revealing experience I took as proof that my life had, indeed, undergone a fundamental change. I had consumed an unusually large amount of alcoholic beverages. I felt excessively light-headed and abnormally over-excited. A film of adhesive material formed on the roof of my head, gluing the top of my brain firmly to the skull. I felt chilly; my eyes glittered unnaturally and my teeth clattered. As I led Julie out and walked with her across the lawn to the car-park, I felt very much on top of the world. Abruptly, I asked her whether she would care to be my secretary. She agreed instantly. Her response was so quick I was momentarily taken aback. I recovered immediately, however, and just as quickly reconciled myself to the exciting prospect. After all, I thought, why not? I was an architect, executive and co-owner of a sizeable business concern. I did require a secretary. The excitement became so pronounced now that I could not quite contain it. I walked without feeling the touch of my feet on the ground: it was as it I was floating in the clouds. Julie, my secretary. That did it.

I was not aware that I was leading Julie to my partner's home, which was located near the hotel, until we actually arrived at the gate. I opened the gate and, holding her hand, led her along the narrow concrete path Khatib had constructed across the small front-yard. It was a modest but impressive little house with a carefully-tended lawn fenced in with a variety of exotic plants. I rang the bell and the door was immediately opened. Still holding Julie's hand, I stepped inside, pulling her close behind me. "My personal secretary". I announced. I was shaking and my eyes glittered with the intensity of insanity.

Amal was in the act of pouring heavy soup onto a plate, using a large spoon. Her hand, holding the spoon full of gravy, stopped in midair as she surveyed the scene. Khatib stood near her. He was holding a flat, wooden utensil dipped into the rice bowl. He, too, stopped to stare at us. Presently Amal, her lips pursed but otherwise displaying no emotion, continued with her task. They were both silent.

I walked to the dining table and seated myself on a chair behind a steaming plate of rice. I then invited my secretary to join me to partake of these other people's lunch. Fortunately, Julie had the presence of mind to dissuade me from further acts of folly. She refused the invitation, pointing out that we had just had our lunch at the hotel. She also insisted on leaving immediately. I forgot about the food and followed her out.

I introduced Julie to my other acquaintances, including Norla and Nadhim. The former was not surprised: she seemed to accept the impression I had encouraged her to form, in regard to my presumed wealth and prosperity, at face value. Nadhim, however, knew me well. He knew that I was not wealthy. When he saw Julie, he understood right away that it was not the prospect of secretarial services that so excited me. His mouth suppressed a slightly pained smile as he gazed discreetly at her well-formed, casually exposed breasts.

Work at the site progressed on schedule. I kept myself busy attending to the requirements of the workmen. Within a few days, the structure that was to house the machinery was completed. A well was dug and labourers' quarters were erected. Our associates in Europe advised us that the machinery had been dispatched and we were to expect it at any time. All was well and going according to plan. I pressed Julie to visit me in my apartment, but she played hard to get. I invited her to more expensive dinners at the exclusive restaurant.

The ship did not arrive on schedule. It did not arrive the next day, nor the day after. My hectic pace lessened. I became restless. I sent urgent telexes to our associates in Europe requesting for an explanation of the delay. I drove to the port and made inquiries in person. No definitive word was given concerning the delay or even the whereabouts of the vessel. I grew more anxious and ill at ease with each passing day. A baffling message surfaced onto my consciousness vaguely suggesting that the ship was not going to arrive. A feverish sensation enveloped my entrails. I felt icy cold and shivery. The moment of truth had arrived; and the long, dismal journey had began.

6

As anxiety built to a frenzied pitch, I felt an upward pull in my head, forcing me to knit my brows in pain. Then I felt leaf-like layers of material being yanked off the top of my head, one at a time, rather like pages being torn out of a book. My eyeballs enlarged and my eyes started to burn fearfully.

I did not know what was happening to me. Vague messages kept surfacing from the recesses of my mind suggesting that I should have known the project would not materialize. In fact, that I had known it all along but had chosen to ignore the truth. I refused to acknowledge the disturbing messages. I grew ever more frenzied and desperate. I tried to get hold of myself and to act normal, but failed. I could not relieve the pressure that was forcing my eyeballs out of their sockets, nor could I reduce the concentrated energy in the lenses that made my eyes burn. I kept trotting about listlessly. Later, there appeared a liquid pressure on the top of my head, somewhat like sandgrains falling on water. As the disturbance increased, the pressure forced my head to bend down.

My illusions of grandeur all but disappeared. Nadhim, a pained expression in his countenance, begged me to go look for work. He offered to accompany me to the employment office to make inquiries. On his insistence, I tried to move myself from his shop with the intention of going to hunt for a job. My legs would not move. I tried again, harder. It was no use: my legs felt as though they were nailed to the floor. Sensing that I was unable to make up my mind, he gave up the attempt. When the idea of looking for work vanished from my thoughts, my legs moved.

Julie sent me a note saying she had to leave town, and thanked me for the dinners. I hardly understood the meanings of the simple message. Nor did I miss her: she had already become part of a dream that was slowly disappearing from my mind.

The following day a friend who was working at the airport brought word that our associate from Europe had arrived. Trying to keep myself calm, the information nevertheless brought fresh hopes surging into my mind. My dreams revived with greater impact than ever before. I had not been taken for a ride after all, I thought jubilantly. Relief flooded in me with such force that I shook and trembled all over. It was as though the man was bringing with him Aladdin's magic lamp. Anxiety built up with renewed force and, intermingled with other emotions, created a mental state of high fever. I spent the morning hours pacing the floor listlessly, waiting for the man to arrive. Several hours later, with the mental fever at peak, word came that there had been a mistaken identity. The supposed associate turned out to be just another pasenger from the flight.

The fresh news just about paralysed my mind. I looked here and there uncomprehendingly, trying to make some sense out of the arrested turmoil in my head. The inside of my head felt like a fluffy ball of cotton. Incomprehension took prominence over the jumbled emotions. A passing acquaintance, noting the imbecilic bafflement reflected in my eyes, suggested that I return to Muscat (our permanent residence was in Muscat. Salalah was only a working station).My mind digested this latest message. I had a vision of our poverty-stricken homestead in Muscat. I saw the narrow, dirty lanes amidst which our home was located. I saw the fifthy, smelly sewage slime that was disgorged from old broken pipes. I saw the greasy pair of garbage drums in front of our home. From the middle of the Cosmos, the awareness came to hit me suddently with the knowledge that I was going to live near filth.

I presented a spectacle rarely witnessed on Earth. My back bent like a bow-string as if to run away from the dreadful sight; my eyes, focussed relentlessly on the fearful image, popped almost clear out off their sockets as I was seized by the most intense terror imaginable. Pedestrians were arrested in their movements as they stared at me in amazement. It was unearthly. But besides the pain, which was pure hell, I also presented a scene of supreme comedy. For there I was, the budding, jet-set millionnaire, abruptly revealing the hidden truth in a single gesture: that I was penniless, jobless, secretary-less, frightened out of my wits and mentally deranged as well. I realised, furthermore, that I did not own a car any longer: the vehicle belonged to my former employers and it had been returned. When I came to think of it, I discovered that I had no place to sleep in: the apartment also belonged to my ex-employers and it had to be returned, furniture and all. In fact, the only possessions left intact, or otherwise undamaged, were my pants; along, it could justifiably be added, with an erect; expectant manhood. But the gem of the humour I was to appreciate only later, when the pain in my head had lessened somewhat.

Thankfully, the horrid experience lasted only a

moment. I feigned a reassuring smile to those of my acquaintances who had witnessed the scene. However, they avoided my eyes, and were far from reassured.

The following day brought no news of our associate. The chill froze my innards. I began to shake uncontrollably with anxiety and fright. The burning sensation in my eyeballs increased in intensity. Suddently, it seemed a bolt of lightening struck inside my head. My knees buckled and I fell on my haunches. Trembling with shock and fright I rose with difficulty and walked the short distance to Norla's boutique. I picked up the telephone and dialled the number of my former office, and requested my former workmate, who pickjed the phone, to get the proprietor on the line. But the man was not in. The next day, there was still no news of the foreign shareholder. Again my brain seemed struck by lightning. Again my knees sagged and I fell down. Again I walked, trembling, to phone my former employer. This time I found him. Urgently, and a little hysterically, I begged the man I had insulted and scorned only a few days back to reinstate me in my former employment: in the job I had pointedly neglected and despised. The co-owner, a dignified head of his clan, politely turned me down.

Now totally hysterical, I dispatched an urgent commercial telex to Adwan—the man I had cruelly maligned —begging urgently for a job at his office is Salalah.

And the second bead disappeared into the dark subconscious.

Our Greek associate, a handsome gentleman in his

early forties, arrived two days later. He brought little consolation to me, however. He knew nothing of the whereabouts of the vessel. He speculated that the ship may have been pirated in the high seas with forged documents, and the ship's name changed and our cargo sold to some underground villains. It sounded like a script for a good sea-drama motion picture. I thought, ironically, that it was quite the appropriate way for the ending of my hollow dreams.

Nevertheless, the Greek was of the opinion that a Government-backed investigation should trace the whereabouts of the vesel and that, ultimately, the cargo should be recovered. His unsupported optimism that all should turn out well in the end was sufficient cause to raise my unreigned hopes and emotions high up again.

I decided to fly to Europe once more just to reassure myself that my dreams were still alive. My inner, more stable awareness forced the truth onto my consciousness, but the surface emotions stubbornly rejected rationality. The two opposing sets of reflexes then locked in a fierce combat. As I trotted stubbornly from the shop to catch a cab to the airfield, the battle in my head became so intense the pressure felled me to the ground. I recovered from the fall and, stubbornly, stopped a taxi and proceeded to the airport. Norla watched me from inside the shop with a quizzical, wry gaze.

I flew to Athens and stayed at the Hilton. (The cost of travel was debited to the partnership account. The hotel tab, including meals, was picked by our associate, as was the case vice-versa.) We made inquiries on our goods and discovered that the cargo had never left port. The ship had not sailed, either: it was marooned at the pier tangled in a host of legal and commercial disputes. I returned to Salalah with little hope that the machinery would ever leave port.

Meanwhile, Khatib and I had other problems besides the stranded cargo. We had built barrack-like quarters with the idea of renting them to one or other of the construction firms. A friendly banker had promised to provide the funds, but changed his mind afterwards. By then the structures had been completed by a local constructor who had built them on credit, and was now pressing for his payment. Other financiers we approached were no more helpful. Khatib had suggested that I sell my shares of this particular business; pointing out, reasonably, that we had a problem on our hands and I was not in the right state of mind to help find a solution. I had agreed to the proposal. This had taken place a day following my arrival from Athens. A day later, with a financial balance of some three riyals in my pocket, I appealed to my partner to advance me a couple of hundred riyals. The inside of my head was now in a liquid state. A persistent tapping sensation disturbed the liquid—rather like a butterfly disturbing a bowl of syrup. In the centre of the liquid there was a slowly-revolving disc—not unlike the signal flag that changed train tracks. As I was anxiously forcing my demand for the loan, Khatib reminded me of the agreement regarding the sale of my shares. I confirmed the agreement readily once again. But as soon as I had stammered the words, the disc in my head revolved upwards. Abruptly, I changed my mind, and told my partner that I was not going to part with a single share of my stocks at any price. Baffled, he reminded me that that I had just confirmed the agreement. The disc revolved downwards. I stammered hysterically that the deal was made and to carry on with the transaction immediately. A moment later, the disc went up. "No", I shouted. "There is going to be no selling of any assets belonging to me. Never!" The discussion came to an inconclusive end.

7

Khatib lent me the money, which I used to repay some outstanding bills at the hotel and a few minor debts with individuals. The major debts, however, amounting to thousands of riyals remained outstanding with the banks. These I had borrowed partly to finance my vacational trips to the Far East, and partly as working capital on one or other of the numerous business ventures. The balance that remained in my pocket now amounted to some twenty riyals. I discontinued taking expensive meals at the hotel. With a friend's help I found a moderately-priced eating place which offered palatable local fare. Within a few days, however, this eating house, too, became too expensive for my budget; my pocket balance had dwindled to some five riyals. There was still no news of the ship, nor was there any sign that the machinery was going to arrive soon—if ever. I now ate my meals at a low-priced luncheonette, which catered mostly for unskilled expatriate workers in the lowest wage-group, located near my former company-provided flatlet which I still occupied pending a formal hand-over. I had no transport now. In the morning I walked to the town centre and ran around in circles until midday when I caught a taxi, that charged on passenger basis, to the cafe. I ate my meals hurriedly and then walked home to sleep.

Balance three riyals. I caught a taxi from the town-centre to the eating house. (It was at the height of summer. The five kilometre distance to the luncheonette was too far to cover on foot, in the oppressing heat, even in desperate need). I got out of the taxi, paid the fare and ran to the restaurant. I ordered a plate of fried chicken and bread. In a state of acute fever, I gobbled the food as though I was in an emergency military standby. Holding the half-burned backbone of chicken in both my hands, I gnawed the skin off the bone-marrows and reached for the bony-roots in the inner thigh with my teeth.

Balance one and a half riyals. My teeth clattered, my limbs shook and my eyesight magnified haphazardly. I calculated that I now had two meals worth of money in my possession; and on which my life hinged. I did not catch a taxi this time: every single baiza was too precious to spend on anything but food. I half-walked, half-trotted in the direction of the eating house. Luckily, my friendly landlord passed by in his taxi and offered me a lift. I ran in desperation to the luncheonette and ordered a plate of mutton curry and bread. I devoured every morsel of fat and wiped the plate clean of any smear of curry with the last sticky bits of bread.

The following day, my financial balance was three quarters of a riyal. The money was sufficient for only one meal, plus the taxi fare. Not paying the taxi fare would not help, I believed, since the balance after lunch would not cover the cost of another meal. I had one meal's worth of money for my life—and then the unknown. I wondered what was going to happen after the last meal. I imagined that I should probably expire in some mysterious fashion. Midday came quickly. After a hectic deliberation I decided that the labourers' cafeteria was now too expensive for my finances. Like a cornered beast. I searched frantically for a way out. I came to the conclusion that the only practical course of action was to prolong my days for as long as possible through the most economical use of the seven hundred and fifty baizas I possessed. Accordingly, I hitched a ride to the far end of the town hoping to find some bargain food to satisfy my hunger for less than what the restaurant charged. I entered a grocery shop. Loaves of bread of various sizes were displayed along with childrens' toys and sweets. I calculated the approximate cost of a small loaf of bread and some canned sauce to eat it with. The cost should come to some three hundred baizas, I guessed. That was more than half the cost of the regular meal. I walked out of the shop. "No", I told myself heatedly. Any reduction of my funds meant that the end was that much nearer.

I placed my hand in my pocket and gripped tightly the two notes on the value of which my life depended, and vowed never to let go come what may. I walked a few paces and then felt dizzy. I felt a sensation of falling as a curtain of fine, colourless cotton dropped slowly from the top of my head downwards. My mind blurred, my eyes dimmed. I swayed and fell on my knees.

From afar, a glimmer of intelligence came to mind that my brother Nabil lived only a short distance from where I was. With this bit of knowledge the curtain lifted a little and vision improved. With considerable effort, I managed to walk the one kilometre distance to my brother's home.

52

Nabil was my eldest brother but one. He was the least educated member of the family. Neither the whipping of the religious teachers nor the gentler prodding of academic educators had ever tamed his wild independence or created an interest in learning. He threw stones at the former and simply walked out of the class of the latter. Father did what any responsible parent would do under the circumstances: he whipped the skin off the wayward brat. Nabil walked out of home. But notwithstanding, he was the most kind-hearted man I knew. When father was away on a trip, Nabil took care of us. I recalled how, with our meagre resources stretched to the limit, he would clean the money-drawer of the last saved pennies to add to the available cash in order to make up the cost of a loaf of bread. He would then go out only to return empty-handed, and coax us to forego our supper. He would make up a story about a thief who had stolen the money. We would discover later that he had given the money to a deformed beggar he had met on the way.

He was now working for a telecommunications company and living in a spacious, company-provided apartment.

I stayed in my brother's apartment and slept all day. At night, I tossed about, lying alternatively on my stomach and back. This disturbance lasted for several days. I thought that the soft-cushioned double-bed had something to do with my restlessness, so I discarded it and slept instead on the less comfortable sitting-room sofa. The excruciating discomfort did, indeed, lessen substantially.

The inside of my head was now filled with stirring emotions. I started to feel, and act, like a child. I opened the refrigerator every so often and helped myself to the variety of candy my sister-in-law kept for herself and the children. Later on, I felt as if the world was running away from me. I couldn't keep still. I felt I had to do something urgently and expeditiously to keep pace with events. When the sensation intensified the chaotic passions in my head then whirled violently in an anti-clockwise direction. I was bombarded by conflicting urges and desires, each directed to a different goal. Something told me to dispose of all my stocks in the business and then travel on an everlasting vacation. This was countermanded by an appeal that I find a job and start working immediately. A third, and equally compelling directive would have me get married. Still other appeals urged for the speedy acquisitions of different, and often contradictory goals. One weak but persistent voice whispered that I disregard everything and simply go to sleep for good. Finally one authority took command.

I rose from the couch, grasped the car keys and walked with certainty, to where the car was parked. It was as if I were being led—or rather, being pulled forward by invisible strings. I drove the car directly, and following the shortest route, to Norla's boutique. I knew exactly what I was going to tell her.

"What do you think of me now, Norla?" I demanded of her as soon as I entered the shop. I was desperately hoping that she still had the same impressive opinion of me. She looked at me impassively. Wry humour touched her wide, sensuous mouth.

Suddenly I said "I am afraid". "Why"? She inquired casually. Then she added, "You have done nothing to be afraid of." "I am afraid of people, afraid of the world, afraid of after I had uttered the words that I knew what I had said;

my life, but had never allowed it to surface onto my consciousness. I knew also that it was the cause of all my past misery and my present torment.

I looked out of the window and saw sharp outlines of structures but poorly defined details of the contents. It was as if I was looking through a pair of small, sharp lenses. The view seemed to crowd on me. I shook with fright. "You think you are the centre of the universe, Maher". Norla told me. I stared at her in wide-eyed incomprehension.

"Are you staying at the hotel now?" she inquired, changing the subject. "Of course not. I can't afford it." "I thought you said you were rich". She reminded me as she bent to retrieve a dress a customer had dropped, silently and politely dismissing my presence as she did so.

Overwhelmed with humiliation, I left Norla and walked straight to Nadhim's shop across the street. I lingered about uncertainly for a minute, not knowing what I wanted to do. I requested a pen and paper and when these were provided I placed the sheet of paper on the table and held the pen in my hand. Then abruptly, and involuntarily, I bent down so that my hand holding the pen was on top of the paper. My mind formed clear, photograph-like images. I saw myself married to Laura and living happily with her in a flatlet on top of an office my brother owned in a provincial town. I saw Laura, shy and contented, smiling in her quiet way and nodding her head at me. And I knew what I was supposed to write. But I also knew that I did not want to. My hand, of its own volition, wrote the name of Carol, the addressee. I forced myself to stop. I did not want to write any more. I knew that what I was about to write was humiliating and revolting and wrong. The compulsion to continue with the writing intensified. For a split second I struggled against the unknown force that was compelling me to act against my will—an act that was clearly base and rotten.

I surrendered in a hurry. I felt as if a vice was squeezing the top of my head until the brain compacted stickily against the base. The sensation was that of a soft nut caught between the jaws of a powerful cracker. I had a distinct feeling that the power that had now taken command of me had met my outmatched, but determined resistance with considerable anger—as if to warn me that any challenge to its authority was not only useless, but was bound to be very painful as well.

I never knew the contents of the letter I had written. But I knew the gist of it: it was a marriage proposal for Laura, the sweet young daughter of Nadhim and Carol whom I had pointedly ignored when everything was seemingly going well for me. The sweet young lady Carol had tried so hard to stir my interest in.

I placed the letter in an envelope and handed it to Nadhim to deliver to his wife. I then left the shop and drove directly home.

The last and major bead in the chain disappeared into the darkness.

Two days later I drove to Nadhim's shop and begged him for a minute of his time in order to talk to him. He was composed as usual. The same sad smile shadowed his well-defined features. He parried my frantic begging, hoping that I should change my mind or simply forget whatever new emergency that had croped up in my mind. I insisted on talking to him. Convinced of the hopelessness of the situation, he finally relented. I led him across the street and up a deserted stairway.

"Nadhim, I didn't write that letter!" I assured him solemnly. I was feverish with anxiety and icy cold, as usual then.

He smiled sadly, a melancholy expression in his clear eyes.

"I—Nadhim, I am insane". I was frantic in my efforts to convince him.

He looked directly into my eyes. "You are saner than I am". He stated with conviction. "What is more", he continued, still gazing into my eyes, "It is not the first time you have spoken on the matter.".

I had indeed made a casual remark on the subject once. It had been a thoughtless utterance. The unfortunate remark had, however, raised Carol's hopes, with the result that her pain and sorrow compounded with the dissolution of their heightened expectations.

I searched my mind desperately for some way to describe to Nadhim the unnatural compulsion that had made me write the letter, if only to spare Carol more pain: I had punished her enough for the crime of bestowing on me her love and affection.

I could think of no way of getting the truth across. I tried to recollect the contents of the letter, hoping to disvover an inconsistency with which to support my contention of mental disorientation. But I could not recall a single word apart from the address. All I could recall was the impression I had when I wrote the letter: that I was conveying a matured desire for matrimony, supported by a responsible statement of my future plans and expectations for the happiness of my prospective bride. It was in fact, the kind of a proposal that could only have been written by a responsible, level-headed suitor with the interests of his fiancee foremost in mind.

No wonder Nadhim believed I had a firmer grasp on reality than he did.

Defeated once again, I permitted Nadhim to go take care of more productive business.

8

The matter inside of my head kept changing into various shapes. Now it was like an incomplete fishing net placed on an even ground—and just as useful. The bundle of the knitted material occupied the bottom half of my head. The top half was empty. My mind now absorbed, sponge-like, any idea, information or a mere suggestion as an absolute truth. Had someone suggested that I owned the Sultan's palace, I should have believed them. Had they suggested further that I enter the palace to take rest, I would have done so. Along with the total loss of reasoning powers, sensitivity to pain also took prominence. I could not stand the slightest mental distress or physical pain. While talking to Khatib about my shares in the barracks business, I cautioned him to avoid arguing with me. In any discussion, Khatib argued pointlessly. He used irrelevant parables to press a point. He querried the warning on my state of mind, pointing out that in a business discussion arguments were bound to occur. He persuaded me, gently, to part with my shares. He also managed to convince me that he was my most sincere friend and brother. He was only relieving me of a burden I could not carry in my present state of mind, and paying substantial cash besides, he assured me. However, his accounting of the merit of the sale was decidedly unpersuasive. Even in my blank state, the hollowness of the transaction as far as my side of the deal was concerned was glaring enough. To have wrestled the argument point by point, however, would have required functioning intellects as well as a markedly resistant threshold of mental stress. I possessed neither. I yielded to his will like a child.

Having discovered how easy it was to overwhelm my resistance, Khatib attacked my other weaknesses. Like a two-faced snake crawling in the grass, he struck with venom where it hurt and then puffed on the wound to relieve the pain. He discovered my pathological fear of the unknown and applied gentle pressure; increasing the pressure gradually to ensure that I remained docile and submissive. Meanwhile he moulded my equally sick, abnormally suggestible intellect to create a firm belief in my mind that he held only good will and brotherly consideration for my welfare. He ever managed to extract a half-hearted commitment for the remainder of my assets free of charge.

When this news reached our financial backer (who owned an equal share), the latter directed that I be reimbursed for the initial planning and efforts put on behalf of the partnership. The amount promised, but not immediately found, was reasonable and fair, though substantially short of the actual value of my stocks. I had not yet signed the actual deed of surrender. A final decision still eluded my mind, in spite of Khatib's maximum devilry.

A steam-jet appeared at the base of my head. The steam shot upwards and then bent in a perpendicular direction to flow within the net, forcing my head to protrude forward. The phenomenon sent to the fore the feelings of profound misery on my predicament, compelling me to solicit the sympathy of every acquaintance I met. Some of my acquintances showed concern and offered mostly irrelevant advice. A few sympathised with me initially, but ignored me when the flow of self-pity persisted. I went to the homes of some of my acquaintances and unfolded my woeful story to their wives. One kind-hearted, talkative wife of a friend sympathised with me the most. She interrupted the flood of self-pity several times to offer her own opinion of my wretchedness. She recriminated me for my envious greed and suggested that it was the cause of all my misery. She advised me never to be envious of the wealthy, but to be contented with what I could achieve, with the blessing of the Almighty. She dissolved some herb in a glass of water. I accepted and drank the yellowish juice gratefully.

Of the few acquaintances I had, one of the closest was Noor; a good-natured fellow who enjoyed a good joke. He held a prominent position in the money market. Noor was always considerate and sympathetic to others' misfortunes, and would go to great lengths to be of help whenever called upon for assistance. I needed his advise on the matter of my remaining stocks and also desired his sympathetic attention. I drove to his office with high expectations that I should obtain both to my satisfaction. As soon as I entered his office, however, I discovered that I wasn't going to get much of anything from him. For no sooner had he seen me approaching then he fell into the most helpless laughter. I lingered about uncertainly in the hope that his mirth would come to an end. Finding myself unable to even exchange a greeting, I left him, still laughing helplessly, and drove away.

I visited Nadhim again and, in the presence of Carol, poured out my lamentations. When she saw me, Carol flinched as though I had dealt her a telling physical blow. She ignored me at first. But when she looked up and saw the wretched, baffled expression in my eyes, she drew a deep breath and then let out the air in a long-drawn out, pained sigh. I saw the changing colours in her white, sunburned countenance as she struggled to control her repressed emotions and to stop the tears from dropping to her cheeks. Her voice quivered as she offered what sympathy she could muster. She advised me to find a psychiatrist to have my problems sorted out professionally. She then bent her head on her paperwork with added concentration. I remembered the letter I had written to her, proposing marriage to her daughter when I was at the end of my tether and had become the laughing-stock of the whole town; the girl I had studiously ignored during the happy times. I left quickly and drove home to sleep.

Unknown to me, my prolonged stay in my brother's house was causing havoc with his foreign wife. I dirtied the place and created a sickly atmosphere in an otherwise bright home full of cheer and laughter. The domestic crisis for which I was responsible had reached a breaking point: my sister-in-law had threatened to commit suicide if I was not ejected from her home. The following day she carried out her threat and attempted to do away with her life. I had returned with my brother from a drive to the market to find all doors locked. Nabil shouted for his wife, but there was no response. He exclaimed furiously that she had probably killed herself.

It was only then that I became dimly aware that my long, sickly presence had not been welcome. I was so closed in my misery I never guessed that anything was amiss. Nabil had tried everything possible to awaken me from my stupor, to no avail. He had begged me to get hold of myself. He had shouted angrily to get me on the move. He had even tried gentle persuasion. Nabil saw every problem as a protruding nail. His one solution was to hammer it deeper onto the wall. I had observed for some time that he drank spirits excessively. I had also noted his overly tempestuous fury and unprovoked temper-tantrums. I never realized that my brother was breaking himself apart on my account. Caught between the love of his family on the one hand, and the deeply-ingrained sense of responsibility for his kinsman on the other, he could not think of a practical compromise. He became frustrated and tortured himself sick instead.

At last, however, following his wife's suicide attempt, he decided he could stand it no longer. Late in the evening he confronted me with a proposal. He told me that whilst I was welcome in his house and, in fact, that he wanted me to stay on, it was nevertheless in my interest that I leave for Muscat to find a job. He mentioned my elder brother's business as a possible source of temporary employment.

I digested the information dimly. "But I won't have a furnished apartment to live in." I objected idiotically. Nabil pointed out that I could survive without a furnished apartment.

"But I won't have a car." I objected again. Nabil pointed out patiently once again that people survived without motorcars. It took me a long while to digest, analyse and finally comprehend the information. It was years later that I realised, that it had been the closest my brother Nabil would go to showing me the door.

I booked my flight to Muscat the following day. I caught a taxi to the airport carrying only a brief-case in which I stuffed what little possessions I had with me. On arrival at the airfield we were informed that the flight had been cancelled, and I returned to my brother's apartment. Both Nabil and my sister-in-law welcomed me back cheerfully, saying that they had both known instinctively that I would not travel. It was only after I had seen the apartment following the two-hour absence that I appreciated the gloom my presence had created: it was glitteringly tidy. The dirty lounge I had left only a while back was scrubbed clean. The atmosphere was already bright and cheerful within a couple of hours of my absence.

I caught the next flight at noon the following day. I left the house early to say goodbye to Nadhim and Carol. I also passed by Norla's shop and apologized to her for the deal I made on the business—which included the boutique—without her knowledge; and explained that my state of mind had been such that I could not do otherwise. I had plenty of time to spare before the departure of the flight and I decided to visit Noor again. I entered his private office unannounced, as usual. As was the case previously, however, I was not able to talk to him. He was seated in his comfortable executive chair. By the look of him, he had started laughing for quite a while before I entered his office, suggesting that the sight of me walking in the street was a sufficient joke to cause him amusement.

His eyes glittered. I prolonged my stay, hoping that his mirth would be exhausted. Instead, it became more vigorous: he began to use his hands—in addition to his mouth and the tearful eyes—to express his humour. He laid them on the table, turned them every which way, placed them beind his head and finally laid his head on them. These activities were in addition to the task of wiping the tears off his cheeks every so often. He did not make a sound. Again I left him without exchanging a word.

I arrived at the airport in good time for the flight. I was holding an economy class ticket, but as I took my seat in the economy class cabin I panicked. There were passengers in the first class compartment and I could not understand how it came about that I occupied a lower class than them. My body jerked forward involuntarily, but I forced myself to stay put. I knew that I was holding an economy class ticket and that I was seated in the right place. I was jumpy and felt increasingly desperate. Panic seized me ever more feverishly. My head shook with gyrating emotions. From the bottom of my head multi-hued clouds formed and moved to the top. Shades of colour represented varying degrees of intensity as well as the quality of pain. The most painful and weird were the metallic-hued sheets of cloud that churned underneath thick layers of fog and shot upwards. These brought an eerie sensation of receding reality so that I slipped further away onto the illusion of insanity. It was the most agonizing sensation yet. As the overloaded plane laboured to attain a higher attitude (in order to overfly atmospheric turbulence) but kept falling back to the same elevation, I gazed at jagged rocky slopes below and half-wished the plane would crash onto the mountains. I trembled with the agitated emotions and felt remorse at the thought of other passengers paying with their lives for my selfish wish.

9

In Muscat I lodged in my mother's home. It was a relatively tidy and modestly-furnished two-room abode located amidst a surrounding of poverty and dirt. My emotions remained disorderly and panicky. I felt like a man about to drown. Streams of flares shot upwards from the base of my head, making me jumpy. Occasionally a powerful flare speared majestically from the chaotic surface to the roof, and I would jump in panic to do I knew not what. I saw everyone's activities as somehow connected with my problems. When helpers in the employ of my brother (who resided in an adjoining homestead) came looking for him to announce the completion of some errand in their business, I ran out to listen to their discourse. I hoped, in my desperation, that their conversation would add up to the speedy arrival of my ship.

All my passions and emotions seemed concentrated on the surface of my head in overcrowded disorder. My senses were erratic: my vision was at times sharply-focussed, causing my eyes to blaze. At other times my vision dimmed and I could make out only very close views. At still different times I saw through half-shaded lenses, as if I were looking through a field telescope.

I was still undecided on the matter of my remaining stocks, despite the verbal promise I had made to give them away. These were prospectively far more valuable than those I had sold. I still hoped for the arrival of the problematic ship before making up my mind one way or other. But I could not stand the prolonged indecision: everything had to be dealt with urgently—or so my impetuous sensibilities directed.

The pressure of desperation finally dictated that I reach a decision immediately. After several attempts, all ending in failure, I snapped a decision at last: I was not going to part with my stocks, come what may. What if the machinery did not arrive I thought. What if the bank held each party responsible to make good the liability? Obviously I could not stand the strain. I decided, a moment later, that I had better forget my pride and bravado and surrender the trouble-plagued stocks. But what if the ship did make an appearance, and the project turned out to be the money-spinning factory we had envisaged? Could I stand the sight of all the accumulated loss, my dreams included?

I could not make up my mind, but the surging emotions dictated that I reach a decision. Slowly I marshalled my will. I was going to make a decision, I promised myself solemnly, and it was going to be final.

I decided to hold onto my stocks and I pledged, that it was a final decision.

The jumbled emotions and passions converged to form a single soft lump. I thought of the construction at the site of our project in Salalah; I saw the image of the factory and I felt the excitement that had preceded the activity. The lump in my head disjointed in the middle:

one half was dismembering itself to follow me with my dreams of a money-spinning empire. The balance half remained stationary.

I flew to Salalah the following day and signed the legal deed for the disposal of my stocks free of charge. Fortunately, the document included the directive of our financial backer regarding my reimbursement. The last link with my dreams had been severed. I returned to Muscat feeling empty and purposeless. Having discarded the dreams I lived for all my adult life, I did not know now where I fitted in the order of things.

My senses of sight and hearing became more erratic, my intellects more haphazard. My vocal pronouncements were involuntary. Instead they exposed the inner truths I should have kept to myself. My limbs felt loose. When I walked, my waist followed the torso zigzagedly, like a cheap whore exhibiting her rear. I smoked ferociously, ate a little food and slept. Anxiety built up with redoubled force: I had a compulsion to do something; but I did not know what it was.

For lack of any constructive ideas with which to occupy myself, I travelled again to Salalah to collect some odds and ends of my effects which were still lying in my former apartment. Nabil offered to carry the luggage to Muscat in his pick-up, and I consented: airfreighting the bulky collection of cheap furniture would have been uneconomical. I also decided to travel by road with him, since my air transportation was no longer gratis. I perched myself in the cramped passenger seat of the rickety truck, my bundled belongings carelessly thrown in the back, and proceeded on my journey home. Uncovered mattresses hung conspicuously on the sides and dirty pillow-cases waved cheerfully in the gentle breeze as we wound our way through the narrow lanes in the central market area. As the journey progressed, I felt a curiously odd sensation of belonging—as if sitting in a cramped place and surrounded with greasy instruments, with a driver beside me, was and had always been my rightful niche in life. At the out-skirts of the town we stopped to re-arrange the luggage and to tie the ropes on top. I felt old, done with and rather tiredly comfortable with the world. We continued with the journey. My recent presumptuous past regressed further away from my mind as we made our way deep into the desert. Then I recalled Julie, and my lips widened in an ironic smile. I remembered that I had already resigned from my job when I asked her to be my secretary. In fact, I had hired her as my secretary when I was myself jobless—and penniless as well. It never occurred to me that she would need a salary for her employment, assuming that there was work for her to do. I started to laugh. The cover-up was so ridiculous and hollow.   I laughed deeply and continuously. Nabil saw me and became scared. He shouted angrily at me to stop laughing to myself. I turned my face to one side and laughed until hysteria threatened to overtake me. Scared, I gritted my teeth and managed, with great effort, to put an end to the laughter.

My mind was a mishmash of dread and consternation as we passed by the odd bedouin hovel in the periphery of the coastal villages near the end of the desert waste. There,

I thought, was where I belonged. My life, I felt with growing apprehension, should always have been in those huts. A peculiar sensation of comfort, mixed with the stirring of fear and dismay gradually enveloped me.

Ramoom was a village of my ancestors. It was a collection of mud huts scattered haphazardly within the perimeter of a field of date plantations and crisis-crossed by narrow tributaries from an underground stream nearby. This was the place where my parents grew up, and where both my grandparents had been born. Many were the enchanting stories I heard in my childhood of the magic land of my ancestors: the juicy fruits that grew from its fertile soil; the adventures of my father's childhood within the surrounding hilly terrain; the clash of armies within the plots of green plantations. In fact, it was a hardy containment of abject poverty, supporting a collection of weather-beaten, withered family of settled nomads which had grown in time to form a clan.

My paternal uncle lived in Romoom; and so did my half-sister, numerous cousins and an assortment of distant relatives from a more or less common lineage. Our journey took us past the marked point where an open, tire-graded path cutting deeper into the hinterland led to Ramoom. Nabil suggested that since we were so near our home-village, we might as well pay our relatives a goodwill visit. Accordingly, he turned the vehicle in the direction of the indicated wilderness. We drove on until we reached a dry river-bed which crossed over the path. This was a juncture that indicated our journey thus far was in the right direction. As Nabil negotiated the vehicle across the river-bed a tire got stuck in the sand. We disembarked to examine the situation. Nabil dug a hole under the tire, using his bare hands, and directed that I collect suitable stones to place in the hole. I felt weak. I barely managed to carry a few stones—when all strength drained away from my limbs and I sat down to rest. Nabil shouted for the stones. Tiredly I rose and walked a short distance to search for stones. As I carried two small stones painfully, I felt that the manual task I was doing befitted me; and that I was suitably employed in my rightful occupation. We managed to extricate the vehicle from the sand and proceeded on our way. We drove past desert bushes and sturdy, thorny trees which grew in abundance in semi-arid regions. The geo-physical panorama was almost a carbon-copy of the landscape I remembered as a child in the village of my birth in Africa. I was really returning home, I thought in growing panic. Ramoom was indeed my home; and the poverty-stricken, dirtily-clad occupants of the muddy homesteads were really my blood-relations. And I was on my way to rejoin them.

A fog of dread and fear closed in on me. I fought in panic for some way of escape. Vision failed. My mind went blank—and I fainted.

When I came to, we were already winding our way inside the village. We stopped near our uncle's home and, as usual, the heavily-bearded old man was most gracious and profuse in his welcome. Gradually my eyes became used to the view. I was, however, in a delicate and infirm state of mind. When I looked at the surroundings, I allowed my eyes to rest only a moment on a limited view at a time, in order to protect myself from possible shock from an overdose of reality

We spent the night at the village and resumed our journey the following day. On arrival at home I asked my elder brother, Hamdun, to hire me to work in his office at Nizwa. I withdrew some money from the bank and handed a goodly sum to his wife as a gift. (The amount I gave my sister-in-law was roughly the equivalent of a three-month income on the wage terms Hamdun agreed to pay me. In fact, I was repaying in advance the wages I should collect from my brother for the initial three-month period of service). I then caught the bus to Nizwa.

It had been a long time since I last caught a public means of mass transportation. Except for the comparatively luxurious rides in tourist coaches, and occasional trips in the underground tubes in foreign cities—altogether different propositions from the common conveyers of mass commuters—I never rode in a bus. Now, as I took my seat in the bus, I felt I was retrieving my rightful place in the stream of life after a very long lapse.

On arrival of Nizwa I was welcomed by an affable Indian youth who looked after the small travel shop. We took a liking to each other at once. Robert had heard all about my misfortunes and he was most sympathetic. I shared his accommodation which was located on top of the office. It was a modest one-room flatlet with simple but tidy furniture. I threw a spare mattress on to the floor and slept on it. I wanted to feel care-free. But it didn't work. I felt only a confounding sensation of misadaptation. I complained of my misery ever more persistently to Robert, who had by then exhausted his sentiments of comfort.

In the evening, I walked to the market place. I entered the dark, narrow alley on both sides of which ancient, bearded vendors sold odds and ends of iron-ware, traditional *khanjars* and cheap, ready-made *thob*. The vendors sat in cave-like booths surrounded by their wares. They chatted with their neighbours and did not appear particularly concerned with their customers. Their primary interest seemed to be to while away the day rather than to reap financial rewards from their occupation. Tentatively I examined some dresses with my fingers and waited for the attention of the vendor. None was forthcoming. I moved to the next cubicle but found the same lack of enthusiasm. I returned to the first booth and inquired loudly for the price of a thob. The man absent-mindedly quoted me the price. It was much cheaper than I expected. I purchased three thobs of different colours, together with an equal number of undergarments and head-covers, and then left. As I walked back to the office I thought, with a narrowing focus of intelligence and a childish, pleasurable sensation of anticipation, that upon dressing in the cheap thob and headdress I should be indistinguishable from the crowd at the market place, and should become as one of them. I would while the time of day within the narrow alleys and crouch in the dark caves and chat with a vendor. I would be one with the common mass of my people with whom I belonged.

I climbed the stairs to the room and I dressed in one of the new thobs. Unpressed and a few sizes too short, it fitted me well in my new role. But I didn't myself fit in: I felt oddly comfortable, but more lost than ever. I felt like a comedian mis-cast in a tragic motion picture. I discarded the garment and redressed in my tailored thob.

I took walks around the town. I tried to fit somehow with the leisurely pace of the unhurried inhabitants, but it was no use: I walked impatiently as though I had to catch up on an important appointment with destiny. I slept with deepening disquietude. My forced adaptation to the unused naturalness felt increasingly illusory and phony.

A friendly youth resided in an apartment below us. He was, like me, a home-coming migrant from Africa. Rashid was a well-adjusted, highly-informed individual who, it seemed, had no business to be at Nizwa doing nothing of substance. The more I talked with him, the more confused I became. Rashid explained to me that he was at Nizwa because he wanted simplicity and seclusion, none of which could be found in the capital. He spoke German fluently, having lived in that country for many years. His English was excellent and his Arabic was much better than mine. He could land a good job in Muscat, if he desired. But Rashid preferred the simplicity of village life. I did not understand his ideals, nor could I make out the possible rewards accruing from a life of secluded simplicity. Nevertheless, his firm belief had a profound if undefined impact on my illusion-riddled mind.

I drove with Rashid to a garage to service his car. As with all garages, the place was greasy, oil-smeared and dirty. Old, broken parts of automobiles were scattered all over the place. The mechanics, wearing over-alls hunched on their knees and, using dirty rags, wiped the oily smudge off the insides of broken machinery. I removed my gaze quickly from the dreary scene and then spotted a gigantic graveyard of broken metal. Heaps of broken vehicles of various sizes and shapes, hung precariously on top of each other. A stirring sensation—somewhat like the dissolution of an effervescent tablet in water—appeared inside my head. I wanted to shout. With considerable effort I stopped just in time. Fortunately, Rashid just then completed the servicing of his car and we drove away.

I had a balance of six hundred riyals from the funds I had withdrawn from the bank. I extracted the small bundle of currency from my pocket. My hand closed on the money for a moment, then it opened of its own will. The notes dropped to the ground like a deck of cards. I made to retrieve the money but my hand would not move. I tried again, but again I failed

Then I thought of my mother and the fact that she could use the money. Diffidently my hand moved and collected the scattered currency-notes. I handed the cash to Robert with instructions that it be dispatched to my mother by the morning mail.

My mind momentarily went blank. The senses—including those of sight and hearing—vanished. They reappeared a moment later with increased intensity. The eyes blazed and the quiet street outside became noisy. Then the senses re-emerged to a more or less former state prior to the distortion. Now the brain, like a lump of jelly, began to revolve upwards. The revolution affected a major portion of the lump. As the turning progressed haltingly, some outer layers fell back to the base. The moving portion hardened and became metallic as it neared the top. But my overriding concern was one of fear: the shaky mental balance had tipped on the wrong side of the scale.

I reached for the phone quickly and dialled the number of the town office. Luckily my brother was in and he picked up the phone.

"Hamdun, I am going insane". I said simply.

The sensation was one of a hard, metallic illusion. I felt alternate compulsions to embrace poverty at ground level and to prostrate myself in prayer. The pain intensified. I opened a bottle of sleeping pills I kept in my brief-case, filled a glass with water and rapidly swallowed some dozen pills. But even as I was gulping the drugs I knew that the suicide atempt was not going to work: fear of the unknown was too powerful in my mind. I hoped, lamely, that the fatal dose of the sleep-inducing drugs would accomplish its deadly task with sufficient speed to outpace the fury of terror from seizing the initiative away from my will.

As I had thought, however, the hope was wishful and hollow. No sooner had I washed the last pill down my throat with the remaining half glass of water than I jumped up and down and I screamed at pedestrians down the street to come to my help. Robert heard the wails and rushed upstairs. He helped me onto a cruising taxi and instructed the driver to dash for the hospital.

I had a disturbing feeling that the fear in my mind was a distinct, vengeful entity, that it had me in its power and was not yet satisfied with my suffering to permit an end to it.

The poison was washed out of my system and I returned to Muscat a few days later.

10

I had never been to a psychiatrist in my life. The impresion I had formed of the profession through my reading and the movies consisted of a long, luxurious sofa where a patient relaxed in comfort as the practitioner the practitioner probed his mind with suggestive questions. The little wooden chamber the plump nurse had led me into did not contain a sofa. Apart from an ordinary office desk behind which a man sat busily scrawling notes in a log book, and a simple armless chair in front facing the man, the room was bare. It could have been any one of the numerous offices of low-level ministerial clerks. I sat on the chair and faced the psychiatrist, who did not look up even as I made my presence known. I waited for him to finish his work, which took quite a while, and then I began to feel silly and out of place. I wondered what I was going to tell him. Should I tell him that I chased third class whores all over the world in a first class compartment of a speedy jet, using funds borrowed from a bank, and that I then hired a good-looking tart to work as my secretary when I was myself without a job. I stifled a giggle. Apart from the incongruity and ludicrousness of the tale, the sole psychiatrist in town was obviously too busy to entertain a present-day phantom of Abu-Nowais. The very commonness of the place and the heat-oppressed out-door environment somehow precluded all but hard facts of life. The doctor was too busy attending to an honest population, hard-pressed to eke a livelihood from the meagre resources in the sun-baked environment to entertain a jocker from the middle pages of the Arabian Nights.

Presently the psychiatrist laid down his pen and closed the log-book. He raised his head and looked up at me with his full attention. Then in a soothing voice he inquired about my problem. I managed, falteringly, to explain about my anxious and panicky state of mind.

I knew that my explanations were far from the heart

of the problem. I was not even able to describe intelligibly the actual sensation I felt of icy hardness and feverish anxiety which, in any case, constituted only a secondary part of the effect rather than a history of possible causes. The man listened patiently. When I came to the conclusion of my narration I felt that he was not impressed. It was clear that he did not think there was much the matter with me. Obviously anxiety and distress were routine complaints of his patients. The psychiatrist then explained to me the ways with which I should deal with the problem: the careful exercise of spatial and time factors to allow for a planned and thoughtful response to a crisis.

I knew how hopelessly off the mark we both were. Nevertheless, I felt soothed by his words. He counselled me to hold onto religious faith in difficult times, and to be always optimistic for an eventual deliverance. In spite of myself, I was greatly impressed by his confident and gentle manner, as well as his depth of wisdom. A middle-aged, healthy-looking and gently handsome man, he exuded an aura of goodness that seemed to penetrate inside me and made me glow with optimism and hope.

I look leave of the psychiatrist feeling I was well on the way to recovery. I walked out on to the busy street leading to the town-centre. It was after mid-day and the summer heat was at peak. I saw a gaunt old man sauntering aimlessly in the sun. Further on, I saw energetic expatriate workers walking rapidly and purposefully within the tightly-packed vendors' market. I smiled secretively. They did not know my secret, I thought deliciously. The gaunt old man did not know that I would also be able to saunter aimlessly in the sun, at the height of summer, without a care in the world. The hectic expatriate workers, too, did not know that I will also be able to run from shop to shop, to buy and to sell and to do all the things they do. I stopped a cruising taxi and, with a smile of anticipation directed the driver to my home.

The compulsion to find a job built up with greater urgency. I felt that only a secure job could protect me from the terrors of the unknown. Early in the morning I caught a taxi to the town-centre. I got out near a newly-constructed, high-rise building and walked to the bank which was located on the ground floor. It was an impressive and prepossessing office. I asked the first official I met to give me a job. Feverish and panicky, as usual, I felt like a fugitive from a maximum-security prison. I wasn't sure that I could handle a pen. The man appeared uninterested in new recruits. He inquired whether I had banking experience. I replied in the negative and he promptly dismissed me. The following morning I drove to another bank. Again I chose only the most prosperous-looking office to look for work. I was turned down once again. Fear closed in on me. I had to find a job urgently in order to protect myself from the obscure menace of insecurity. But I could think of no other employer with an adequate measure of prosperity to provide me with the iron-clad protection I felt I needed. My eyes blazed fearfully as I walked aimlessly in the direction of Hamdun's Office. I saw bright, distorted outlines of buildings, which appeared to lean forward menacingly. I walked on, passing by the make-do brick enclosures in which budget-conscious expatriate workers lodged in groups. I saw through a window of one of the lodgings which was lit with an electric bulb despite the glaring sub-light—a row of dirty apparel hanging on nails all over the wall. If only I were like them, I thought in despair. If only I had the will and independence to have a place of my own similar to their's, and to hang my dirty clothes on the wall for everybody to see without a care in the World.

I entered my brother's office and lingered about aimlessly. The employees and curious acquaintances gazed at me with apprising looks. Hamdun gave me some blank airline tickets and requested me to write them. I forced myself to complete two tickets and I almost collapsed on the table: I stayed put until I had recovered my strength enough to walk home unassisted and then I took leave and walked out. A former acquaintance and workmate of short duration cruised past the office in his car. As he saw me he reduced speed further in order to greet me. I recognized him, and I also recalled that he had landed a good job with a major airline. I shouted at him to give me a job; and added further, at the top of my voice and with eyes blazing, that I was an ass.

A drilling-like sensation now appeared inside my head. The top of the head was the point from where I could make out the sensation, but it was clear that this was not the starting point. I knew what was happening: my thoughts—or whatever it was—were making the long journey from the centre of the heavens back to planet Earth and onto my head. When the undulating stream hit target, the sensation was painless. When it lost way, or otherwise deviated from its path, my head became foggy and hardened in ratio with the time-lapse. My slippery hold on sanity would slide further away from reality. During one of such deviations—which was the longest—my lower jaw turned violently to one side. The mouth became misaligned, with the upper jaw falling on the lower one at an angle. I put my hand on top of my head as if to arrest the pain. I prayed and begged the Almighty to keep the drilling sensation going. Over and over again, I read silently the religious verses I had learned in my childhood. The sensation resumed. But when I neglected the prayers for a length of time, the deviation recurred. I resumed the prayers, and kept praying for hours on end until I was totally exhausted. I allowed myself some relief from prayers only when the stream fell on a straight line and I felt that a deviation was unlikely to occur.

At night my mind projected eternity: an image resembling a constant scene in a motion picture moving in quick motion, like a cinematic projection of infinite space. It was the opposite of the sensation I had earlier, when I felt the world was running away from me. Now I felt that I need not hurry to do anything: I had infinite time at my disposal. The adjustment of the mental clock went on through the night. The quick motion of infinity lessened, halted, reversed, stopped and moved rapidly forward again. I fell asleep whilst the activity was going on. I woke up early in the morning with a somewhat stable mental equilibrium-except that I saw myself a little taller than a four-storey building. I also felt slightly chilly. I borrowed my brother's car and drove around. I was able to estimate the relative distance between objects and I manoeuvered the vehicle through dense traffic. Mabruk, my eldest brother whose vehicle I drove, had more reason to be convinced that there was really nothing wrong with me.

The sensation of abnormal height adjusted after a long, slow process that took several days. When I came to normal height, however, everything else went askew. Memory blurred. The senses of vision and hearing went awry and my sense of height swung up and down. Later in the evening, I lost identity. I stood on the narrow lane adjacent to our home and stared at the pedestrians who passed by at regular intervals. I wondered who they were, whence they came and where they were headed for.

I walked to the end of the lane overlooking a crowded shopping area. A man walked rapidly past me in the direction of the crowded street full of evening shoppers. On a reflex, my body started, as if to move with him at the same quick pace: I thought I was him. Just then another pedestrian walked leisurely in the opposite direction. I now thought that it was more likely that I was the leisurely pedestrian. A group of shoppers holding parcels in their hands and followed by their youngsters walked by at a regular pace. I did not think it was likely that I belonged to this strange group. Baffled, I walked hurriedly home.

11

The next day, the inside of my head felt dark and empty. I could not stand to be alone: I felt like a shell that functioned when lit from within, with the source of light extinguished. It was impossible to be alone: devoid of the light that made me functional, I felt extinct. I kept close to my brother Hamdun at all times, and felt my body drawing strength from him. When he was taking a bath, or was otherwise engaged in his room, I lingered about listlessly and waited for him to come out. I separated from him only to go to sleep. The sudden and abnormal attachment to my brother did not endear me very much to my sister-in-law. Her thinly-veiled mockery turned to open scorn.

As I lay in bed and waited for the oblivion of slumber to relieve the simmering ache in my head, extraordinary mental phenomena kept on happening. My memory went forward, and then halted uncertainly. Then it reversed a lot faster, and stopped. Again it moved forward much further in time and space than before.

It was like a tape unit, right to the click of a stop button which I heard distinctly. When the tape moved forward, my mind was a blur of motion. On reversing I could just glimpse at disappearing images. The movement was, however, too fast to make out what the images represented.

The reel apparently reached the forward end. It halted with somewhat uncertain finality, as though the momentum continued but there was no more space for movement. I felt a sort of whitish emptiness. Then it rewound rapidly, and I glimpsed at impressions of fast-moving images. The rewinding process took a long time. Finally, there was a blank emptiness.

Vision dimmed until it disappeared altogether. For weeks I could not move further than the adjacent home of my brother Hamdun. Its re-emergence and gradual improvement was equally slow and time consuming. Upon recovery I ventured out to the shops. I entered one and marvelled at the flood-lit items on display. I looked around for an inexpensive item I could purchase for personal use. Just then a group of Indian shoppers entered. I stared at them: I did not know what manner of creatures they were with their clean trousers and huge belts around their waists. Frightened, I picked a small item on display, paid for it and hurried out.

I felt a swaying sensation—rather similar to the sensation one gets aboard a small vessel in the sea bobbing gently against the tide. I had an urge to hide in a hole like a rat. Later I felt a strong need to travel to the village of my ancestors, carrying with me an iron bed, a sack of rice and a cooking stove to secure myself against possible starvation. The swaying motion formed into a scale which moved slowly up and down. I told Mabruk (who always kept close to me, and followed my movements with deep concern and distress) that I had decided to travel to our home village to live there. The scale then rose upwards proportionate to the fall. I felt bold and heroic. I told Mabruk that I had now decided to travel to Canada to pursue my fortunes. The subsequent movements lessened progressively, just like a balancing scale. I made a decision to travel to Africa when the scale fell the second time, and to Europe when it rose. Then I decided to move to the poorer district of the town and to the city centre, respectively.

The scale finally balanced and I decided to stay put. Shortly after, my mind again appeared to settle in place, and the volatile passions steadied.

Everything, in totality, that my mind accumulated in the course of my life laid bare on the surface of my brain. I saw every minor event that had ever occurred in my life as clearly as a picture slide. And I saw the truth, a sort of waning brilliance that illuminated the entire spectrum.

It should have darkened it.

So grotesque and weird was the truth of my life, exposed on the surface of my brain, the sheer unpalatability of it vanquished me. My life represented a paradox that staggered the imagination. I flinched as I beheld the injustice, the pointlessness, the random cruelty of it so vividly exposed in my mind. Fate had tricked me out of a lifetime that should have been rich and rewarding, and had punished me with almost insane fury for a crime perpetrated by unknown forces over which I had no control. To all practical purposes, I never lived, except to suffer frustrations and heartache inherent in a benumbed mind plagued with obscure afflictions and sensitivity, prior to the ultimate punishment. I saw a lifetime wasted in pursuit of false and joyless escapades when genuine bliss I longed for so avidly was within my grasp, if only a mental impediment had not blinded my eyes to it. I saw a life that had never come near another human, had never known the shared affections of friendships, had never felt the warmth of female companionship—except for fleeting glimpses which served only to reveal the magnitude of the loss.

For weeks I lay in bed, dazed and dumbstruck, and marvelled at a freak accident of random chance that was as close to impossible as to make no difference. That the fall when I was an infant should have instilled in me a pathological fear of people and the environment, instead of causing some physical injury. That I should have been present in the room at that particular time when my brother Gamal was examining his stupendous wardrobe and preening himself, at an age when my mind was able to absorb the contrast between us but incapable of differentiating the factual from the fallacious. That my romantic notions should have been so rudely snuffed out at that particular juncture in my life when I was leaving the country for good and would neither have an opportunity for a second try nor for another occurrence that could have rectified the misconception.

Fear bred hatred, which in turn created a maze of conflicting passions. Counter-balancing these destructive forces was a guilt-ridden consciousness which caused the compulsion for self-punishment. The phobia of poverty and dirt complemented as well as aggravated this condition: I came to admire but also hated those who possessed greater material rewards than I did: they represented the glamour of my idealistic relative I had a pathological desire to match. I despised those who fell below me in terms of material possessions and tidy appearance: they mirrored my hidden self. Since I held a firmly-rooted belief that I was poor, I threw money away. I despised the fair sex, believing that they were cheap, whorish and unromantic. But I had a strong erotic drive and I neded sexual fulfillment. The reaction from the repressed natural need for human contact directed me forcefully toward the weaker sex, for the obvious reason that they appeared less capable of causing physical harm. And thus the throw-away largesse benefited those females who charged for their favours, on the sick belief that they represented the only genuine category of womanhood. The outcome from so many improbable maladies was as odd and painful as it was hilarious.

I saw wasted years that had never been put to use: eyes that looked but never saw. A mouth that could speak but almost never did. A mind that functioned but was at a stand still. As a result, I was never involved. I never even returned a smile from an admiring female, of whom there were many.

It might have been fun, had my life taken a normal course. I recalled the teenager who had admired me so innocently long ago, at a hotel in Nairobi. I was to become an object of admiration from so many other members of the fair sex, young and old, and a good deal in between: the young female tourists in Cairo I caught gazing at me with an awe-struck, yearning look in their eyes. The numerous local and foreign women who kept smiling at me mischievously in the streets; the gem of a beautiful woman artist at the Acropolis in Athens, who stopped drawing sketches of the archaeological ruins and, instead, kept looking at me and then scribbling with her pencil on the drawing paper. She showed me the sketch she had drawn: it showed the bewildered pause I had struck seated on a broken pillar from the dawn of history, my head bent down in meditation, the acquiline nose crowning the handsome countenance as well as, I thought, the height of artistic talent. The woman laughed and tried to develop a discourse. But I shied away from her, the way I shied away from all others.

Instead, I paid a pimp half the charges for female company and then waited in a dark corner for a whore who never showed up, as was always the case. On the rare occasions when I did get a woman, she slept like a sack of potatoes as soon as she saw a bed and I kept vigil all night waiting for her to wake up so I could have the long-awaited sexual relief. By the time the whore stirred from sleep it was early morning and I could wait no longer:

nature's demand for rest would exceed the physical need for sex, and I would fall asleep. The woman would then wake up and demand for her money. I would fumble sleepily for the hiding place under the pillow where I kept my wallet, pay her and tell her to keep the change. I would also invite her to order breakfast, which would be included in my hotel bill. Many a whore I provided with bed and breakfast, and paid them for an experience I never attained. I always wondered why it was that the women I found were always such heavy sleepers. The realisation never occurred to me that by the time a whore had caught up with me, she had beaten the streets so hard for so long that her overriding interest right then was a long, undisturbed rest.

There was a time when I did find satisfactory female company for a short period. It was during one of my trips abroad. The sheer number of card-holders made it almost impossible that I should fail to find a woman: had I failed to find one, they would have found me. I was nursing a drink in one of their many places of entertainment when I observed a strikingly attractive young woman. I waved twice, so there would be no mistake. The girl came and joined me for a drink and, afterwards, agreed to come to my hotel. For the duration of my ten-day stay in the country, we kept close together. Besides the love-making—which was too hectic to have really been ecstatic—I enjoyed the togetherness immensely. The love-making, however, occupied most of our time together. I would fall asleep on top of her and the next thing I knew, as I stirred from slumber, was that I was making love. Sometimes I woke up to find myself moving laboriously up and down.

It was at a dance, though, that I had the most rewarding moments of my recollection. A popular song that was the craze in those days was playing. I temporarily forgot my debilitating self-consciousness and I danced with my companion. For the five-minute duration of the song I was one of many people having a good time. I didn't feel awkward and I danced well. We jabbed at each other playfully as we pranced. I observed that other dancers, too, admired us. But for once I did not care what others thought. I felt confident and at peace with myself.

When the number came to an end, my partner simply had a few minutes of a good time. I had five minutes of bliss I should treasure for many years.

Other glimpses at the joys of living included a stroll through a tree-lined avenue with my landlord's daughter in Cairo; a candle-lit dinner with a casual female acquaintance; a chat with my kid-sister while listening to a sentimental song we both liked as we relaxed in the garden of our brother's home, with a light breeze stirring the leaves of citrus plants. But for these scattered golden moments, my past might just as well never have taken place. My regrets were not merely on account of lost time. Rather, they were due to the sublimity of wasted pleasure: if prancing with a simple prostitute could produce so much pleasure, how wondrous the feeling would have been in the company of a loving wife for a stroll in the woods; a walk across a garden path; a candle-lit dinner; home-keeping and a shared bed. The wasted years ought to have overflowed with the very essence of life.

I might have gotten married, had I known what it was all about. I never really gave the matter much thought. As far as I was concerned, the idea was too fantastic to be real.

Vaguely, I thought of marriage as some kind of a deal that would allow me to indulge in as much sex as I wished with an agreeable female under contract. I saw married people, together with their wives and children. But the sight made little impression in my mind. People were only vague phantoms with whom I had little in common.

The closest I came to understanding marriage was with Amal and Khatib. Amal had more than a hint of sexiness with her although it was mostly hidden in her dignified bearing. I failed to see her marriage as involving sex, however, due to the pronounced unhandsomeness of her spouse. I knew and understood that they were married, but I fell short of fitting the sex part in the arrangement. To do that I would have had to swallow the fact that the unseemly hypocrite pressed his member on royalty, and that the latter accepted and liked it. The idea somehow upset my scale of values. My mind would rather accept the incomplete picture, and I lived comfortably with it. Carol, on the other hand, though desirable in every respect, did not attract me sexually. So I did not connect her marriage to the gentle Nadhim sexually. As for Norla, who was attractive her marriage was not near enough for me to wonder what went on with her husband at night. There were no other couples in my life close enough to interest me to examine marriage in its proper perspective. So the childhood disillusion with the fidelity of the opposite sex remained unchanged.

I saw the years I wasted trying to discover the elusive feeling that something in me was struggling to be freed. I kept wondering what it could possibly be and what I could do to encourage its manifestation. I wrote stories, hoping that the elusive feeling would surface somehow through my writing. I wrote the most unutterable rubbish and I though I had created outstanding literature. My world was confined within the orbit of my own wild dreams. Nothing that other people did had any significance, and everything that happened to me was magnified. Merely to utter a word was an adventure. On the rare occasions when I made a witty remark, or told a joke that was appreciated by others, I savoured the moments for years and I felt tingling thrills whenever I recalled the memories.

They were miserable years of soul-searching: the perpetual meditations; the concentration on my hectic writing. I concentrated so hard trying to squeeze from my benumbed intellects some substantive ideas for my stories I almost collapsed by the time I wrung out some worthwhile notion. I would think, in a frenzy of excitement, that I had conceived the brightest thought in literature. I would be so exhilarated I felt smothered in the tempest of creativity. I would then wear my outdoor clothes and walk stiffly, in the dead of night to a library that kept late hours. I would gaze at the volumes of books on display and the sight would sober me: nothing I could possibly acomplish would compare with the monumental works in front of me. With this humbling thought I returned home to sleep.

I used to feel sick almost daily. There was a perpetual pain on one side of my tummy, and a throb in my chest was a persistent irritation I learned to live with. I would wake up a few minutes before the opening of the office, brush my teeth hurriedly and then walk to the office. I day-dreamed the hours away until the office closed and I hurried back to sleep. The routine went on for years, interrupted only to travel for the vacation. But even during my stay abroad, I followed the same routine—except for a few minor distractions. Sometimes I broke the routine to visit a company doctor. I would make an initial visit and then follow it up with regular visits for several days, complaining of multiple illnesses. The physician attended to me patiently for a few days and then, convinced that there was nothing wrong with me physically, he grew impatient and irritable. I caught him once gazing at me with a contemptuous look following a mock application of an injection: he had nicked me slightly with a needle when he was supposed to have made an incision with a syringe to administer the medicine. I realised only much later that of course he had not injected me: he had simply pricked my skin and charged the company ten riyals.

When I went again to see the physician a week later with a brand new complaint, he dismissed me, saying that the illness was in my head and not in my limbs. He was right, that one time.

12

One day I cured myself of all my ailments. I had neared the climatic conclusion of a simple story and I strained the over-wrought sensibilities beyond endurance. The inflamed passions ran amok and I collapsed onto the bed. I feared that I should die before I completed my narration (a piece of nonsensical conjecture unworthy of the effort of a ten-year old, but which appeared in my mind as a work of brilliant imagination).

As I went to sleep the fear intensified and I became profoundly miserable. An instinct for survival prodded me to fight for dear life and I kept repeating to myself, with the full force of my will that I was not going to die. Sleep overtook me with my determination intact. I woke up early in the morning feeling very healthy, active and free of any physical complaint. The throb in my chest vanished and the pain in my stomach disappeared. Energy bubbled in my limbs so profusely I wished there was somebody with whom I had had a quarrel in order to settle the matter with a fist fight. I ran to and fro within the small backyard to be rid of excess power, but the excercise did not suffice: energy flowed into my limbs steadily, pressing for release. I thought of provoking some innocent pedestrian into a fight, but discarded the notion for fear that the man could use a knife instead to settle the quarrel. Then I thought of the one time room-mate and frequent visitor who was a thorn in my flesh with his pestering and teasing. And I really allowed that skinny little shrimp to make a misery out of my life, I thought in amazement.

It was about time for the opening of the office but I decided not to report for work. Instead, I was going to hunt for my vexing visitor to settle a few scores. But then I remembered that I did not know where he lived or where he worked, and I gave up the idea. The physical soundness was a unique phenomenon to me: I had never felt so healthy and energetic before. As I walked slowly in the direction of the office I began to wonder whether all was as it should be with me: a pain that had troubled me for years could not just vanish like that, I worried. I concentrated to feel the reassuring pain in my tummy. Gradually, with hard concentration and increased fretting the pain reappeared, the heaving in my chest resumed and I was myself again.

And that was the life I had: a life of self-denial and penance. The uncanny part of it all was that there was no-one, and nothing to blame. The little maid who had dropped me to the ground when I was an infant was not to blame. An image of a little girl came to mind. She should have been around fourteen, although I did not remember thinking she was that old then. She was grinding corn using a long, smooth wooden trouncer with which she pounded the grain stowed in a bucket-like wooden container. I was around six. It was hot and humid and I was sitting idly with a young houseboy at the rear of our homestead where the kitchen was located. The little maid would pound the corn a few times and then raise her skirt playfully to exhibit her bare bottom at us. He smooth little behind was drenched with sweat which reflected the sunlight, making her oily black skin glossy. I felt strong erotic urges but I didn't know how to go about to satisfy them. My little companion asked the girl to allow me to indulge in sex with her and pointed at the store-room where we could hide ourselves. I felt nervous, however, not knowing how the performance was done. I was also apprehensive lest my father catch me in some mischief.

Some half a dozen years later, on a visit to my home village, a young woman approached me. Giggling shyly, she inquired after my health and that of my parents. She also wanted to know how we were doing in our new home. I did not recognize the young woman but I did feel a distant familiarity with her. As usual I shied away and wished the woman would leave me alone. She prolonged the one-sided discourse with inconsequential inquiries and I became less and less forthcoming. Finally, giggling with pronounced embarrassment, she said goodbye. I thought that there had to be a strong bond between us for her to act so forwardly with me. Generally, tribeswomen shied away from public displays of friendliness with men. I understood now that she was the little maid who had accidentally dropped me. The poor girl was not to blame for the fateful mishap. Nor could I blame my mother for entrusting me in the care of one so young. Accidents occurred. All children fell to the ground at some time or other in the course of their upbringing. I could have fallen from my mother's own loving embrace. The little maid had loved me, too, as the recollection showed.

Certainly, I could not blame my brother Gamal for owning better clothes than I did. Still less could I blame the village girls for charging two pence for their favours. Thus, not only did I not have any outlet for the pain, there was nothing tangible against which I could direct my anger. I could not very well vent my anger on mere chance. And so I led a life aloof and separate from others. I loathed and despised humanity because one of their members, in whose protection I was entrusted, failed me and dropped me to the ground. I bought new and expensive clothes in order to dirty them and then throw into the gutter. I spurned true affections and sincere friendships and chased false glamour. Ultimately, I threw my battered life, too, into the gutter—as had happened—the same way I disposed of used and dirtied apparel. I spurned Amal's and dear Carol's affections the way it hurt most in order to punish myself the most, later on I despised and insulted my employers so that I should subsequently lower myself the most. I spited Adwan maliciously so that I should be despised by all. When, after months of total negligence of my job, I found satisfaction in the few minutes I worked, a part of my mind was warning me not to despise my means of livelihood and the source of my bread. But I ignored the warning, as was always the case. I exhibited Julie in front of Amal and Nadhim in order to inform them, in the clearest manner possible, that I was low and despicable and was not, therefore, deserving of their affections. My desperate efforts to impress Norla with wealth and refinement were motivated by the urge to have not only Norla and her husband, but the entire expatriate community they were in touch with to discover me for the impostor I was.

I saw now that I had not been waiting for a ship to arrive in Salalah: it was the actual act of waiting that I was waiting for. All my life, I had waited for something or other. In my school days, I waited for a cheque from my brother Mabruk to arrive.

While working I waited for the holidays to come. In my stay abroad I waited for a prostitute to wake up from sleep. And everyday, I waited for the manifestation of the mysterious feeling that something in me was amiss. In fact, I had been waiting for the return of my fabulous brother Gamal—or, rather, for my transformation into an image of him.

So vivid was the exposure of the whole truth in my mind no practitioner of psychiatry could have made it any clearer.

Someone interrupted my broodings with the news that our neighbour's daughter had given birth to a baby-boy. I had been in the same state of infirmity when I had heard the news of the girl's marriage sometime back. So at least nine months had passed since the onset of the illness. I was still a helpless invalid, and there was nothing I could do about it. I could not go to work because my faculties had not as yet returned to normal, and also due to lack of energy. I did not go to the hospital because I could not explain what was the matter with me. On the other hand, if my intellects functioned properly, I should not need medication since I should be sound and well. But I could not explain this to my people, who kept nagging me and insisting that I do something to help myself. To be able to do anything at all, including making a simple explanation of my helplessness, I needed reasoning powers and a properly functioning mentality.

The knowledge that I had money in the bank shook my head with such force that I disposed of it promptly: I gave it to Hamdun as a long time loan. When the intelligence sank into my head that I no longer owned a penny, the shaking ceased. Light-headedness set in and I began to ramble once again. I recalled the names of all succesful businessmen in town and I said that I, too, should have been as succesful. Whenever a familiar name was mentioned in connection with some achievement in life, I said that I, too, should have achieved as much. When someone mentioned that a relative of ours had purchased extravagant furniture, I said that I, too, should have owned expensive furniture. For want of something to do, and also in order to get a respite from the ridicule of the household, I found an excuse to travel to Salalah once again: the reimbursement I had been promised by my former partners had not yet reached my bank. I flew to Salalah and drove to Khatib's home where I met Amal.

She seemed much her usual self, but quieter and somewhat reserved. If she felt pain and loathing for the depraved malice I had brought on her she did not show it: her dignity was intact. I apologized profusely for the wrongs I had done her and I begged insistently for her forgiveness. Lamely, I tried to describe the strange forces which had compelled me to humiliate her the way I did. But the forced explanations sounded hollow and ludicrous even in my own ears. I would have her believe that I had been sick and, as a result of the sickness, some mysterious power had compelled me to hire a secretary I had no conceivable need for—except, of course, for the obvious—and further that this peculiar power had also directed me to exhibit the shapely tart on her face. The explanation did not even convince myself, despite my certain knowledge of its factuality. It sounded preposterous and impossible. There was no such disease!

13

I went to meet Khatib in his office. As I walked the short distance from the car park to the Ministry compound I knew that I still had a long way to go before I even began to think of going to work: my limbs were uncoordinated, my eyes were expressionless. The view of the surrounding appeared blurred, mysterious and frightening. I entered Khatib's office, sat in a chair like a faithful dog and waited for the explanation regarding the delay of the remittance; knowing instinctively that I should only hear lies, but not knowing how to deal with the situation. Khatib noted the idiotic expression in my eyes and he lied easily and confidently. He told me that the funds had since been transferred to my bank and that I should find the deposit in my account upon my return to Muscat. He did not even know the bank I did business with. But I was too dim-witted to discern even the obvious. Seeing that I was swallowing the lie uncritically, as usual, he became confident enough to show me just what he thought of my idiotic trust in him: he smiled widely with a closed mouth, dropped his eyelids half-way on his eyes and removed the expression of intelligence.

His nasty sly eyes now reflected not only scorn, but contempt as well. But I could not fathom the reason for his contempt. I returned to Muscat and checked with the bank regarding the remittance, but I was informed that no funds had been received in my account. I thought there had been some unforeseen reason for the delay and did not worry about it.

I decided that it was about time I went to look for work. I asked my mother to wake me up early in the morning. However, when the time arrived I was unable to get out of bed: I felt heavy and feverish with the need for sleep. I told her I couldn't go out that day and I went back to sleep.

A while later, (or so it appeared) I heard my mother shouting at me to wake up. It was presumably another day, but the need for sleep was even stronger than the previous day. Some basic process was now taking place in me, but I couldn't guess what it was. The voice subsided as I fell heavily into sleep. Sometime later I heard from afar insistent and angry voices trying to wake me up. The shouts faded as I slipped further into oblivion. I began to understand what was hapenning to me when I sensed what I believed were the remaining sparks from the extinguishing flame of life. There were four sparks. Three sparks. Two sparks. It was like a tick of a clock announcing New Year's eve—or doomsday. I could not see; I could not speak; I could not hear; I could not move and my memory was blank. No other sensation was discernible. But for the remaining one spark, my mind was empty. There was nothing I could do, nor did I know how to prepare or brace myself for the last spark which, I was convinced, should conclude my life. I could not raise myself,, nor could I shout for help. In any case, there was no time. Last spark..:; and then immediately another spark ignited so that there were two sparks almost simultaneously. Three sparks—four. I breathed a sigh of relief.

I slept in a huge double-bed which happened to belong to my mother: I had moved to my mother's bed when the need for sleep was most acute. Some two days passed before I was able to leave the bed for supper which, for me, consisted of the soft middle of a thin slice of bread with butter and a little tea. I could not eat anything more substantial. Immediately after the meal I climbed onto the bed and went to sleep. A day later, again in the evening, I ate two soft slices of buttered bread and drank a full cup of tea. On the third day, following a meal that was slightly more solid, I lingered in bed for a while to watch with interest a cartoon programme that was showing on the T.V. When the show came to an end and an adult programme appeared, my faculties were strained, my eyes hurt and I immediately lost interest.

A couple of days later I could walk to the adjoining bathroom to wash my face. I felt heavy and awkward. I wished that somebody, preferably my mother, would wash my face for me. But I resisted the impulse and dabbed my eyes with water. My vision was greatly diminished. My hearing was equally feeble. The following day I ventured into the sitting room. It was dark. I was frightened and I returned quickly to my mother's room. A day later the darkness no longer scared me and I moved to sleep in the sitting room.

I lost weight and my sensibilities improved progressively as the days passed. On the evening of the seventh day I felt a strong urge for a cigarette. I felt so dirty I thought my face had been used as a home for a spider and the grimy remains were still stuck on it. I thought of changing my dress before going out to buy cigarettes (I had been wearing the same thob for at least the past two months) but I could not summon up the energy to do so. I walked to the toilet intending to wash my face. But my hand would not touch water. I tried to turn the water-tap: my hand moved only a little distance and then, on a reflex motion, moved back on its own and hung limply on my side. I moved nearer and tried again, many times. It was of no use: my hand obeyed my command and moved, but recoiled and jerked to my side just as I neared the water-tap. There was some water in a plastic bucket under the tap and I tried to reach for it; but the result was the same: my hand would not touch it. Then an idea came to me: I was going to deliberately fall myself down, knock the bucket in the process and have water cascade all over my body. A stern, instinctive warning cautioned me not to try it. I dared not challenge the grave mental warning, but I did wonder at the possible consequences were I reckless enough to do so. I was convinced that, at the very least, the water would have burned my flesh.

Across the narrow lane facing our home a neighbourly gentleman owned a shop. Amer, whose son was a close friend of Hamdun —(with shared interests in some minor business enterprises) and whose daughter, Nabila, was friendly with my kid sister, felt it his duty to prod me to go to work. He believed unequivocally that there was nothing wrong with me. Whenever I walked to his shop, which was often, he reminded me that time was passing, that every second in a man's life counted and that there was absolutely nothing to make me idle. As I walked out to purchase the cigarettes I passed by Amer's shop. I did not wish to make my purchase in his shop although it was nearer: I was a ghoulish sight; and the last thing I wanted to hear, in my state of acute depression, was more exhortations on the merit of work. But there was no question of resisting the force that was guiding me, against all my instincts and desires, to go there: an entity other than my consciousness was giving instructions to the nerve-centre that controlled movement, and the instructions were obeyed. My own communication with it was switched off.

I walked unwillingly, but resolutely into Amer's shop. I was a frightful sight: the thob I was wearing had been on my body for months on end. My face had not been properly washed for weeks. But the dirtiest part was in my own mind. I entered the shop and there, perched on a high stool and looking gorgeous in a splendid evening gown, was none other than Nabila, the beautiful unmarried daughter of the shopowner. Such was the contrast between our respective appearances I felt anything but a dignified member of the human species.

I handed Amer some change, collected my purchase

and left hurriedly as the two of them exchanged sympathetic glances. I felt rather than saw Nabila's eyes following me out and noting the dirty trousers which protruded shoddily underneath the outer garment. Curiously, I felt a flood of relief and a sensation of delicious deprecation in the knowledge that I had uncovered my true self; and I was proud of it. The spectacle I had presented was bound to stimulate juicy gossip in the neighbourhood for a long time. The fact somehow augmented my satisfaction.

Nabila's presence in her father's shop at that crucial moment when my phobia of dirt was exposed at its pathological worst, coupled with the fact that I was compelled to enter the shop against my will, made for yet another coincidence that stretched logic thin. But by then logic had ceased to have any bearing to the endless mystery of my experience.

My mind broadened gradually. With each passing day my vision and hearing improved, my scope of understanding widened and my intellects firmed. In effect, I was growing up. It was a slow, tortuous process made unbearable with the agony of helplessness against the persistent recrimination of the well-meaning but ill-informed benefactors. Unable to fend for myself, and totally helpless, I suffered unprotestingly Mabruk's insistent nagging that I find medical help. I suffered Amer's persistent pontifical assertions that there was nothing wrong with me and I should start working. I suffered the mockery of my sister-in-law and assorted kin. I suffered the stares of the children in the street who kept hearing about me and my novel incapacity from their elders. I suffered the sarcasm of the neighbourhood tough guys. I reached the apex of my tribulation following a visit by a neighbourly youth of slight acquaintanceship. Ramzi believed in doing good deeds: he always made himself available to assist everyone he thought could use help. Following in the footsteps of his father, who was a pillar of conservatism and communal allegiance, he believed that anyone who strayed from the mould of accepted norms required quidance. As he took leave after the casual visit, I offered to accompany him some distance to his home. We walked silently for a few minutes, covering about a kilometre, when I began to feel afraid that I was venturing too far into the night. Then Ramzi talked. He said that even though he understood that I expected my relatives to continue to feed me, it was nevertheless in my interest to start working. The work, he explained—in a manner that an adult would use to persuade a child to see reason—should help me to forget my troubles and the past misfortunes.

I almost choked in my desperation to squeeze from my feeble intellects an explanation that would describe my utter helplessness and to assure him that it was not free feed that kept me idle. But my strenuous efforts brought out only laboured incoherence. Ramzi nodded his head several times to emphasize that he understood. I persisted in my hopeless eforts at explanations, making less sense the harder I tried.

The youth sighed, as though exasperated that I should try so hard to explain the obvious. He stressed that he knew it all.

It was about noon of the following day, as I lay awake in bed, that I wondered at the night visitor's pronounced interest in my idleness. We were not particularly close.

Then I remembered that the youth was related to Mabruk's in-laws. Why, the gossipy old woman probably made me and my idleness a daily topic of backbiting and vilification. The gossip would start at suppertime and go on and on until late at night. I did make for a delicious subject of gossip, I conceded fretfully. I also made for the kind of topic that would interest the old lady the most: she would harp about my refusal to work, of how I forced their son-in-law's kindheartedness to get free food. She would tell of all the efforts, time and money Mabruk had wasted in order to educate me, and how I ended up a useless leech incapable of earning my bread.

It was a factual, savoury point they would only love to drive home.

Suddenly, I had had it. I was seized by a fit of maniacal, absolute fury and loathing of my tormentors. My head shook. My innards burned with demented rage and my blood boiled. If only I had my finger on the press-button of an atomic device, trained on Mabruk's in-laws, neighbourly shopkeeper and all.

It proved a futile, useless exercise: I had no way of defending myself against my detractors either verbally or through action. I carried the mind of a child. I was incapable of reasoning. I was incapable of action. I could not run away. My eyes saw only vague outlines of the surroundings and my mind could not make out what the view represented. I could not commit suicide: my child's intellects did not comprehend such a complicated scheme as self-destruction. I could not hit my head against the wall in frustration: my shrunk mentality did not understand such apathetic acts of grown-up men. I could not cry.

Mine was the kind of prison that only Nature could

have created to banish a convict. The only thing I could do, in fact, was to grin; and the more telling the pain, the wider the grin. Just then Mabruk entered the house. Frustrated now with my endless inertia, he shouted, in a voice choked with emotion, to someone in the house his conviction that there was absolutely nothing wrong with me.

And I grinned some more.

14

A fortnight later I was able to walk the three kilometre distance to Hamdun's office. It was during one of these walks when I felt a delicious tingling sensation in my groin. I felt childish and shy; and very erotic. I thought of taking a job then: the same type of work I did before. I thought of the teasing things I should tell the girls on the telephone and I imagined their giggly responses and protestations on my advances. As I walked on homewards I passed by a newly-constructed block of flats. From afar the knowledge came to mind that the cozy little apartments could be rented and a home made of them. I imagined how blissful it would be to make a home in such a place. I did not know it at the time that I had reached puberty.

There was no let up to my suffering until the regrowth phenomenon came to completion and I was my adult self again—and after all the mental impediments were peeled off my system. It took several weeks. My mother, hitherto tolerant of my infirmity, and to whom I clung for protection from the hostile world, lost patience. Piqued by my now habitual self-disparaging prattle, she shouted at me to stop raving like a sissy. The noise thudded onto my brain, jolted it and threatened to disintegrate the fragile bundle. The pain stung like a powerful lash on bare skin.

I started as the realization sank home that I knew nothing about my mother, save for the fact that she was my mother. Shaken with remorse, I became aware that I had ignored my mother the same way I ignored all humanity. I rarely talked to her; I seldom listened to what she said and I never sympathised with her when she needed consolation.

For my indifference and folly, Fate saw to it that I atoned—with interest. For having discovered that I was helpless, my mother kept alert for any gibberish I uttered and then pounced on me with avenging wrath. And the penalty for the wrongs I had done her was exacted to the maximum. Meanwhile, demands were made on me to act when I was incapable of action. Reason was forced on me when my rational faculties were in disarray and I was incapable of response. My frantic efforts to describe my angst, and the cause of my helplessness tended only to compound my frustrations: forcibly wrung out of malfunctioning intellects, the painstaking exertions produced only tenuous ambiguity which, if anything, substantiated their charges that I had really no cause for complaint. So long as I didn't flap my hands like a bird and try to fly into the air, or carry a long stick and go to direct the city's traffic at midnight, no one would believe that I was mentally ill.

I kept wondering why the pain-relaying stimuli did

not get blunted, or some controlling system become overloaded, break down and cease to transmit pain. But in contrast to all the other unruly sensibilities, the mechanism for the transferrance and distribution of pain performed flawlessly, and with marvellous efficiency.

For a few more days followng the latest ordeal my sanity lingered precariously on the border between reality and illusion. I became highly suggestible and tended to reflect the disposition of whoever I came in contact with. I would feel comfortable in the company of a well-dressed man who had the appearance of prosperity with him. But my emotions reacted violently when faced with an image that mirrored the exposure of my true self. When a close relative from Ramoom came to pay us a visit, my sensibilities ran amok. The man was shabbily-clad and kept an uncared-for growth of uneven beard around his chin. I was alone with the guest. He talked of ordinary matters and I listened quietly for a while. Then abruptly unbidden words poured forth from my mouth: I told him that life in Muscat was very tough; that we were poor and miserable; that we had a hard time feeding ourselves and he should, therefore, expect no food from us! As I spoke my legs stretched jerkily of their own accord. When I finally exhausted myself the poor man, deeply embarrased, took leave immediately. He did not even wait for the customary sweetmeats and kahwa.

I ventured out of the immediate surroundings and I discovered that the sight of the unfamiliar views disturbed my mind. My eyes became heavy and misty when I saw new faces or activities different from those I was used to. Any conversation that dealt with a topic other than my ordeals disturbed my unhabituated faculties even more.

I went to visit a friendly physician of long practice and I described to him as well as I could my mental regression and the consequent regrowth. The doctor explained that psychiatry was not his speciality, but he guessed that I had been suffering from hallucinations and delusion. He went on to say that while the functions of the brain had been charted and were fairly well understood by the experts, the mind as such remained in large part unexplained and that no one had claimed to fathom the workings of the human mind.

I wrote a brief on my experience to date and handed a copy each to the psychiatrist, the friendly physician and my brother Mabruk. The latter read it and pronounced that I had been suffering from a nervous condition. He dismissed my illness as though it were little more than a slight headache a couple of aspirins would have taken adequate care of.

It was a bright fine morning a couple of days later when I woke up early feeling a little light-headed but sound both physically and mentally. I pranced about in the sitting room. It was a ridiculous manner of celebration for the tortuously-earned freedom; nor did it impress my sister-in-law's brother who wanted to know what the jubilation was all about. I explained to him that I had finally recovered from the long and incapacitating illness. "There was nothing wrong with you." He informed me self-assuredly. "You just thought that you were sick."

I walked out into the street and looked about. I saw a newness to everything. I went driving with my kid-brother and I marvelled at the sunny freshness of the vendors' market. When we stopped at a grocery shop for soft drinks, my little brother chatted with the shopman. I was dumbfounded: the kid talked with people as though it was the most natural thing in the world. It then dawned on me that of course talking with people was the most natural thing in the world to do. Tentatively, I put in a sentence, too: I asked the man how his business was doing. I half expected to be ridiculed. But the man brought forth a long narration of how his business had seen better times and of how, suddenly, everything had come to a standstill. He hoped however, that business would start moving once again soon, with the Almighty's help. The long story dazed me and I took my leave immediately.

There were no invisible strings pulling me away from human contact now. However, I felt no particular inclination to talk to people although I knew that I could now do so with ease: my affliction had been too vague and hidden for me to appreciate its absence.

Near home there was a little cafeteria and I decided to have my lunch there. The place was tastefully furnished and attractively decorated with plastic carvings of marine life. I ordered rice and curry which I ate with a healthy appetite. The bill was a quarter short of a riyal. A quick calculation showed that I could have fed myself at least one good meal a day—which was more than what I had been eating when I was sick—for about two decades with the money I had in the bank. If only I had known that there was such a thing as a restaurant, I should have saved myself a world of grief.

In the evening, as I walked along the main road, I saw well-dressed women, their hands knotted around their husbands' folded arms, strolling within the shop-studded lanes. Momentarily I was flabbergasted: I did not understand how it came to pass that pretty women walked with other men. Instinctively, I wanted to shout at them not to be fools. But then I remembered that of course I did not own all the women in the world. In fact, that I owned nothing at all.

I decided that it was about time I started working. However, I had a little business to take care of first. I inquired with the bank regarding the reimbursement that was supposed to have been remitted to my account by my former business partner. No funds had been deposited. I called Khatib and reminded him of the matter, and he reassured me that the funds had been transferred to my account. When I asked him which bank my account was supposed to be in, he was rattled but he managed to wriggle away with a lengthy harangue on the intricate functions of the banking system. Khatib's lies were so transparent I began to wonder whether he really meant to cheat. More likely, I felt, he was simply submitting to a compulsion he could not control.

I flew to Salalah and immediately made further inquiries at the bank Khatib told me had affected the transaction, to give him the benefit of the doubt. Having ascertained the lie, I went to my brother Nabil to spend the night. In the morning I entered the kitchen and examined the cutlery. From a drawer in the cupboard I fetched a long, razer-sharp meat-cutter and took it with me. I had lunch and then I drove to Khatib's home. Amal opened the door and let me in. She informed me that her husband was not as yet home. She talked to me much as usual, but with a gravity and sadness in her manner which had not been there before. I offered to leave and return later but she said I could wait as he was expected anytime now. I sat down and waited.

Khatib made his regal entrance soon after. We exchanged greetings from afar and then he seated himself at the opposite end of the room. He looked at me for a long moment. Suddenly, he was all humility. I mentioned conversationally that he had been late coming from work. He smiled meekly—as though he was tottering under the heavy burden of wordly affairs—and replied that the demands of work so dictated. Amal placed a plate of rice and curry on the table for her husband and then retreated unobstrusively to the bedroom. Khatib rose and walked to the dining table. I followed and sat near him, and I helped myself to a piece of banana Amal had kept for his dessert.

"I have been to the bank," I informed him unnecessarily. "You have not remitted the money".

"Your money has been transferred to your bank, " he stressed insolently, even now when he knew that I knew he was lying, "Who ever told you otherwise," he went on unashamedly, "does not know anything".

There was no way I could straighten the matter reasonably with him. He had probably convinced himself that he did, in fact, remit the non-existent money. My only alternatives were either to break his skull open, or to acknowledge that I did, indeed, receive the imaginary finance.

I reached my hand under the table and drew out the shiny blade from inside my trousers. "You are lying, Khatib". I told him sternly. "And I have come to kill you"

As I might have guessed, the sight of a knife squeezed the stubborn insolence off him like so much paste from a tube. He rose awkwardly, muttering incoherently, and ran through the back door. He had committed a grave mistake that could have gotten out of hand and cost him his life: he had given me the upper hand and nullified my options. I could neither back down now nor laugh off the bad joke. I was left with no alternative but to carry on with the farcical assassination attempt. I ran after him, and then stopped to stare in fascination. He was running rapidly, but attentively down the three concrete steps to the ground. He ran quickly through the narrow footpath he had constructed across the yard. He skirted around the plant-enclosed fence, mindful of stepping over and damaging young shoots. It took him several minutes to run the dozen paces across the yard; a distance that, for a man running for his life, should have been covered in less than half as many seconds.

He got over the fence and kept on running. His cupped hands beat the air behind him—rather like the oars of a racing canoe. He covered little ground. He ran around to the front entrance and re-entered the house, calling excitedly for Amal to open the bedroom door for him. I stood uncertainly a short distnce but out of view of the bedroom door, and heard the fugitive shouting to his wife. I waited until he had safely enclosed himself inside and then I went and banged the door, shouting at him to open it. From the telephone extension inside I heard him talking to the police. He talked for a long time. Apparently the police officer pressed him for an explanation on the identity, and his relationship with the would-be killer; and I heard the latter as he spun a new web of lies. I banged the door some more and then I walked back into the sitting room, sat on an arm-chair and waited. Soon I saw policemen on the grounds. I opened the door and invited them inside. I was laughing somewhat hysterically. I was hand-cuffed and then forcibly led away.

15

I spent a couple of days in custody at the police station and I appeared in court, along with Khatib, on the morning of the third day. The structure housing the court chambers was imposing on the outside. Once inside, however, the appearance of severity was less marked. A lone, elderly sentry, who gave an air of bored resignation, kept guard seated on an armchair near the door. An old man, with a sizeable growth of white beard sat behind an ordinary office desk perusing, with difficulty, a single sheet of hand-written paper. Another clerk sat near him writing notes with studious concentration. The judge, to whom the sentry directed me, sat behind an unpretentious table at the far end of the room. The former was relatively young. He sported a black beard a few strands of which were turning grey. I sat on a bench close to the judge and waited. Khatib, who had sat on an armchair sideways and seemed to expect the privilege in view of his official post, hurriedly joined me upon the judge's polite but firm directive.

Khatib stated the charges, omitting what was detrimental to his case and emphasizing points which were favourable. When my turn came I had nothing to say in self-defence. I mumbled some words to the effect that I had been mentally unsound for a long time and that I was still recovering from the ordeal. The judge noted sympathetically my insanity plea, which was substantiated, somewhat reluctantly, by the complainant. Nevertheless, he was angry that I had intruded into another's home and taken the law in my own hands. He then asked the complainant whether he was prepared to forgive. The judge had framed the question in such a way that he conveyed his expectation that the accuser would forgive. Not to have forgiven would have meant several years of imprisonment for attempted murder. But I was not really worried that Khatib would withhold pardon: he knew that I never meant to harm him. He also knew that he had provoked me excessively with his stubborn lies. Massively self-assured now that he was in the presence of sympathetic law, Khatib shook his head sagely as he pronounced—in a solemn manner that conveyed the unique nature of his generosity, and for the world to take note of his outstanding act of mercy for the brotherhood of man—that he granted his forgiveness. He reminded the judge, however, that he expected the court to take disciplinary action against the accused, as was judicial custom. I looked at my accuser; the long, shapeless nose that jutted out of a narrow face and the malevolent glazed eyes, and a feeling of pity came over me. The poor man possessed little with which to carve his niche in a competitive world. Common hypocrisy and a profusion of lies remained his only weapons against external threats. I could have sworn that the likes of him had long become extinct. One obviously remained, and just as obviously, if curiously, prospered. He probably felt heroic that he had cheated a mental invalid out of his possessions.

Having exacted his penny's worth of revenge for the ridicule he had been put into, Khatib walked with stately dignity out of the court-room. The judge then pronounced a three-month prison sentence as the court's penalty. I thought he was considerate and fair: a worthy and reliable man for the responsible job of ministrating the cause of justice.

The court sentry led me to a waiting van. I was hauled onto the vehicle and dispatched to the town prison.

I thought it ironic and fateful that I should spend the early days of my newly-acquired freedom within the confinement of a real jail. My days in prison were not particularly distressing. But neither were they a picnic. We didn't do much, so it was mostly a matter of return to our cells for lunch. The luncheon consisted of relatively well-cooked rice with either mutton or fish curry. I ate with a healthy appetite. We were also provided with dessert once every so often and a quantity of cigarettes once a month.

My mother came to visit, and so did Carol and her husband Nadhim who smiled sadly, at me. Poor, dear Nadhim, he could not understand why anyone who had everything going so well for him should have gotten into such a sorry mess for no apparent reason. But then neither could anybody else. Indeed, the quagmire I had fallen into was incomprehensible, and certainly not on account of a three-month prison term. Nor was there an easy way of untangling the maze of paradoxes that brought it all about, and translating it into comprehensible ideas. Had I been able to do so, I should have produced a story of rare beauty. If I could only communicate in words the volume of a lifetime of loss, on account of an obstacle that need never have hindered the achievement of fulfilment—on the contrary, it should have enriched the gain. If only I could have described the depth of the regrets upon the discovery of the cause of the loss, and the ultimate awareness that it was my ignorance of the sickness rather than the mere presence of it, or its causes, that was to blame. I could not help but fall into an imbecilic stupor as the wasted years unfolded and the magnitude of the loss projected itself forcefully. I saw how I shook with excitement merely by sitting beside a pool, under a shade of woven palm leaves, admiring the water and the flowers or when I ventured onto peaceful and clean surroundings or when I viewed, for instance, scenic landscapes. To be near a woman was a mind-bending experience. Little overcoming boredom. I started to look at people as distinct individuals and I learned a little about the lives of others. Most of the inmates were there on minor charges having to do with traffic violations and illegal possession of liquor, and their sentences ranged from a few days to several months. A few, however, were convicted of more serious charges. These wore uniforms with red bands at the back. One disturbed youth was convicted of murder: he had shot dead a taxi driver who, he believed, had overcharged him. Another had shot dead an innocent man to even a family score. Yet another, an officer in the army, had shot dead several of his men on account of insurbodination.

Early every morning we mopped the premises with water. The chief warden would always attend, ostensibly to supervise the work, but in fact only to joke with the inmates; a practice that seemed calculated to make the simple daily chore even simpler with the humour. The wardens carried out their responsibilities unpatronizingly.

A few were friendly. Others simply performed their tasks dutifully. None was hostile. Occasionally we were taken out·of the premises to do outside work. The task consisted of cleaning unwanted vegetation from near the pavements, using our bare hands. Again, the chief warden made it a point to come out and supervise. He would joke with us and cajole the lazy ones to keep pace with the others. When uprooting the grass, I would look at it and marvel at the beauty of the green leaves. I felt as though I was a pupil at school back in Africa. The close-up view of young plants had a slightly dizzying effect in my mind, so I made only cursory examination and enjoyed the soothing greenness. Long before the sun became oppressive the chief warden would call us off the grounds and we would wonder that when Julie agreed to be my secretary, I left Earth altogether. Such transports of ecstasy were due to illness, but they were no less pleasurable for it. If only I had known of my pathologies, and had either tamed the beasts somehow or adapted myself to them, I should have had little cause to be rid of them.

16

Despite the wildness I felt following the disappearance of the mental obstructions, I hadn't really found freedom: I merely exchanged one form of restriction for another. I had only to recall how I suffered the collective stares of the entire staff at the bank when I looked away from them for a moment. When I returned my gaze to the counter, the lot abruptly bent their heads on their papers with feigned studiousness. And how I would enter a room full of chattering people who abruptly became silent; and how they resumed their gossiping awkwardly as they realized that my feelings were hurt. Whilst walking in the street, fingers were pointed at my direction for the benefit of those who weren't aware of my case.

Not much of freedom, that. Given a choice with my former affliction, it would probably be a toss up, at best. In fact, I broke through an internal prison, suffered the tortures of hell and then fell onto an external one no better off than the original. All this on account of the most outlandish, improbable connivance of events imaginable.

But the sequence of singular occurrences was not confined to the original set of causes. The uncanny coincidences following the flare-up of omnipotence was no less mysterious. At every step of the way throughout my illness, coincidences occurred persistently and with such precision in timing as to thoroughly befuddle the mind. Reason could be prodded to accommodate only so much mystery, and no more. That the project which caused the explosion of the psyche should have coincided with Laura's summer vacation. That Amal should have communicated to me her affectionate welcome for closer bonds with her family during the same period. That Julie (and this was the most untenable coincidence of all) should have flown to Salalah, without a really sound reason to warrant the expenditure she could ill-afford, at that particular stretch in time after the psychical exposure, and following the maximum manifestation of Carol's hopes and Amal's expectations but just prior to the actual demonstration of insanity. That I should have encountered Adwan, of all people, just at that particular moment when the beads in the organic chain, that linked my consciousness with the inner mind, were at their most prominence. That I should have been directed to enter our neighbour's shop at the exact moment I shed the pathological sensitivity to dirt, to find the attractive daughter of the shopkeeper perched on a high stool like a bird of paradise. They were altogether too many coincidences, too pointedly suggestive and so aggravated my misery that I could not dismiss them as mere incidents. In my heart of hearts, I knew they weren't. But neither could I categorize them, short of bringing to account the slippery presumption of the supernatural.

Forgive me, Amal. Forgive me, Adwan. Forgive me, world. Do forgive me, Carol. May you and yours never know real pain, except through reading the pages of a book.

The most remarkable coincidence of all was the chance encounter with the disturbed old woman at the psychiatrist's clinic. Her bizarre mirth conveyed much to an experienced mind, as mine obviously was. Just as a knowledgeable musician could distinguish a distinct note from a piece issuing from a divergence of instruments, I could distinguish the clashing emotions conveyed in the outburst vividly; and perceived the texture of the passions as well as the varying degrees of their severity. Pain constituted the predominant emotion. Weirdness and profusion of torment, woven with a queer rejection of the injustice made for the quality of the passion. Disbelief and revulsion, overlapped with a sense of humour at her grotesque predicament, came a close second. Desperation and an urgent need to communicate her anguish to others followed. A sense of futility and the acknowledgement of defeat completed the composition of the unnatural scream.

Hers was pain beyond the normal. Its quality included passions other than the natural. Compared to her, I thought, probably not even I knew what real pain was. She must have been uncommonly goodlooking when she was young, I ruminated idly: that was obvious from the shape of her features even in old age. Her childhood was spent in the peaceful environs of a sunny tropical setting, far removed from the strains and stresses of fashions and modernity. It was hard to conjecture the kind of misfortune which could have brought about her sorry condition. There was only one manner of mishap that could have caused the old woman's baffling malaise: a trick of fate.

Her name could be Tuma. She lived with her mother and aunt in a one-room brick tenement. After school, Tuma spent her time running from one house to another. She would overhear a remark or a delicious bit of domestic gossip which she would then relate laughingly to her mother and aunt. Fatu, her aunt, knitted her hair. She would spend a long time weaving it. Fatu knew that her niece was the prettiest girl in the neighbourhood. She took extra care to knit her hair and felt maternal pride in the knowledge that she had contributed her share in enhancing Tuma's beauty. On completion of her pleasant task, she would spank her niece's little bottom affectionately and then say, with mock severity, "There. Now go catch the fireflies". Tuma would laugh and then run off to the neighbours' homes.

But Tuma did not catch anyone. Nor did she allow anybody to catch her. Whenever a neighbourhood boy approached her she ran like lightning to her home where she hid, laughing, behind her mother's sizeable posterior. Tuma was a swift runner: she outpaced even the big boys in the neighbourhood. She never knew why she shied so from contact with males. She never thought of it. She didn't even know that there was anything amiss in her behaviour. People came to her mother to propose Tuma's hand in marriage. The suitors ranged from old men with broken, tobacco—stained teeth to the youthful and handsome. Some of the old men spoke only jokingly, to humour the women. Others said if half seriously, and waited for the woman's reaction before proceeding further. If her reaction was serious, they tackled the matter seriously. If she took it as a joke, they would stress that they had only intended to be funny. To all suitors the woman had the same reply: her daughter was still too young for marriage. She said it with an encouraging smile to those she considered suitable as prospective sons-in-law. To others she spoke the same words, but without enthusiasm.

Tuma was only eleven. She thought little about marriage; but she knew that this was the subject of the discussions the numerous men held with her mother. She also knew that she was attractive to the men. Every so often, when there was a football match, a crowd of men from the surrounding neighbourhoods passed near her home on their way to the football ground. Almost without exception every man's gaze fell on her. Some smiled leeringly. But most looked at her with only fatherly admiration. Tuma's curiosity about sex was aroused when she spied Mwada with her new husband in their bedroom. Mwada was the daughter of the querulous neighbour across the street. Tall, very dark and very pretty, Mwada always got married. Some husbands stayed in the marriage bond for only a few days. Some kept up with the marriage for as long as six months. Whenever a husband disappeared, another almost immediately appeared. The current husband—a short, tough man who wore his shirt unbuttoned and always dressed in shorts—had been married to Mwada for about a month. He did not live in the same house with his wife, but he came often. Sometimes he came in the evening and left at night. At other times he appeared during the day and disappeared a few hours later. It was during one of his day time visits that Tuma observed the hectic activity from an open window. She burst out in merry laughter. The lovers were startled. The short man awkwardly disengaged himself from Mwada and stalked angrily out of the room.

Mwada's mother was furious. She bustled out of the house and walked rapidly to Tuma's home, shouting all the way. She adjusted the colourful garb around her enormous waist as she trudged. She pushed the door open and shouted angrily at Tuma's mother, saying that Tuma interfered with her married daughter's privacy. She related the incident indignantly. But Tuma's mother was also indignant. She said that they were both mothers and had therefore both experienced the pain of child-delivery. She stressed that Mwada was by no means better off than Tuma, and that the latter was free to go and look where she pleased. It was up to Mwada and her husband to secure their privacy, she pointed out. The offended woman argued heatedly that the big window on Mwada's bedroom—which faced the street—could not be closed during daytime since it allowed the sun-light into the house. If they closed it, she continued furiously, they would require extra fuel to keep the lamp burning in daytime. The defending woman, however, was not impressed with this argument. She maintained that their economics was not her concern: either Mwada secures her privacy or suffers Tuma's incidental mischief. Whereupon tempers flared uncontrollably. The neighbours came and drew the fierce women apart. The male congregation then held discussions with the view to finding a solution to the couple's day-time privacy. One young man suggested helpfully that they use his secure bedroom, when the need arose during the day, for a small fee. After due deliberations, however, the proposal was rejected on the ground that it would prove bothersome to the couple. It was finally agreed, on majority consensus, that Mwada and her husband find another hide-out within the house for their day-time love sessions. A delegation was dispatched to survey the interior of the house and to suggest a suitable site for this purpose.

But for the occasional quarrels with their neighbour, Tuma's family was peaceful and serene. It was also remarkably free of worries. There was no permanent provider of food, but they never went hungry. The relatives who sold vegetables in the market-place brought fish and vegetables. The male admirers of Fatu also brought food regularly; and there were the visitors from the clove plantations who brought quantities of oranges and vegetable to spare. Tuma's mother would sell these to obtain the cash for other expenses. When a religious festival approached, and the family had no spare money to buy Tuma a new dress, Fatu came to the rescue. She would adorn herself in her best festival dress, wear her shiny necklace and ear-rings and, together with a female companion similarly attired, walk to the ocean-embankment. They would wear purdas also, but these only hung loosely behind them, leaving their frontal parts free of the veil. The purdahs signified their respectability, so that. only well-dressed men of equally respectable backgrounds dared approach them. They would accept offers of ice-cream from suitable admirers and they would converse with them. Late in the night they would walk leisurely back home. Two handsome men would follow a few paces behind. Sometimes they did not find suitable gentlemen to follow them. In the event, and depending on their need for the money, they would stroll leisurely in the main shopping district. All the shops were closed, but they would admire dresses behind the display screens. A passing motorist would then blow his horn and inquire whether they wanted a lift. The women would accept.

Tuma's father, Sumani, sometimes came to visit. He was a man of small stature, given to eccentric behaviour. He wore a pair of pantaloons that had many folds around the waist, and the leg-lengths hung considerably short of his ankles. He had married Tuma's mother for only a short period and then disappeared when she gave birth to Tuma. He spoke some English and he sometimes worked as a guide to occasional European visitors. He brought a present for Tuma whenever he came to pay a visit. Occasionally he would also bring a slice of mutton for his one-time family. Before handing a present to his little daughter, he would make a face and say that he had heard that she was naughty. He would fetch a rope—which he kept for that purpose—and then he would pull and half carry the struggling girl out in the open. He would tie her leg with the rope and secure it against a lamp-post. He would then fetch a stick and administer to her mock beatings. Tuma would yell and laugh in turns. Finally he would untie her and hand her the present and she would run to show it to her friends.

Fatu and the elder woman would exchange amused looks. They knew that the man simply wanted to remind the neighbours, as well as to inform curious passersby, that he was the father of the pretty little girl.

Tuma shared the only room in the house with her aunt Fatu. When the latter brought a male guest, she slept in the open with her mother. In Fatu's room there was a big mirror under which she kept her cosmetics. Another, smaller mirror hung on the wall. Tuma often looked at herself in the mirror. She would open her mouth and examine her strong, even and shiny teeth. Tuma brushed her teeth every day using a soft branch from a tropical plant. Often, she would feel a vague urge to do something, but she never quite understood what. She would linger about in annoyance and then find herself walking into the room to look at her reflection in the mirror.

17

Years passed. Tuma grew quieter. She no longer ran from one neighbour's house to anothr to overhear gossip. Instead, she did the house-hold chores. She also cooked sweet beans in heavy syrup which her mother sold in cupfuls to pedestrians and the neighbourhood children. In the evenings she wore her festival dress and, together with her aunt Fatu and a neighbourly acquaintance, attended marriage celebrations, which took place all the time. They would sit on a mat and clap their hands as an old man sang teasing praises of the bride, with strong sexual connotations, to the accompaniment of drumbeats. The song said that the once proud maiden, who never looked at a man, had fallen into the clutches of a sexual brute; and it advised the bride not to feign a headache in the course of an active night. The hand clapping women would laugh hilariously. The song then turned to the bridegroom and advised that he, too, should not complain of exhaustion in case the seemingly reticent bride turned out to be more than a match for him. The clapping women greeted the suggestion with uproarious applause.

Naza was a quiet youth who lived in a large house opposite Tuma's home. His family was relatively prosperous, owning a number of vast clove plantations. His father also had a steady and well paying job in the Goverment. His office was located in the 'wonderful house', so called because it was an imposing three-story structure of novel design. It also had a lift. Naza always sat on the raised concrete platform attached to the house, which was constructed for that purpose. Sometimes his father and the children joined him; and together they enjoyed the evening breeze. Naza smiled at Tuma whenever he caught her eye. Once he showed her something in his hand and then called on her to take it. Tuma was curious to see what it was, but she felt apprehensive and could not come close to him. He put the article on his knee and folded his arms on his chest. She drew near uncertainly; but then she demanded that he closes his eyes as well. As he did so, she darted forward and picked up the present quickly. She then withdrew to a safe distance and examined it. It was a simple dress ornament.

Naza opened his eyes and smiled at her. Shyly, she smiled back. He then unfolded his arms slowly. Tuma watched as he kept his open palm on his knee and invited her to hold it. Tentatively, she approached again, reached for his hand and touched it lightly. The pupils in her eyes glittered excitedly at her daring. Slowly, Naza moved his hand from his knee. Her muscles tensed. She stood erect, ready to spring like a wild impala at the first sign of danger. But the youth made no effort to grab her. He caressed her hand lightly and inquired whether she planned to go to the sea-shore that evening. Tuma said that she didn't know. She giggled and turned sideways to see whether the neighbours were witnessing the scene. But there was no one about. Naza held her hand and pressed it. Abruptly, she detached her hand from his grasp and moved rapidly away.

During the night Tuma stayed awake for a long time and savoured the strange sensation of yielding to a man's will. With the possible exception of her father, she had never come so close to a man before. She didn't understand what the actual sensation she had felt was: it had been neither defined pleasure nor pain. But she knew that it had been overwhelming.

It was at the seashore, late in the afternoon as she kneeled on the ground, her hands scooping the wet sand when a youth, his swim-suit dripping with water, walked resolutely towards her. Tuma had observed the youth eyeing her frequently as he trotted to and fro along the beach. But unlike many others, who gazed at her with open, if slightly flirtatious admiration, the youth was grave and did not display undue interest in her. His gaze was frank and did not waver as he inquired politely, but firmly, where she lived. Tuma giggled and nudged her campanion, who rose and, together, they walked way. She was to see him again a few weeks later. Early one morning several neighbours, including her mother, converged at Naza's home to help with the cooking for a party of guests from the Royal House. Lambs were slaughtered and a big feast was prepared. When the guests arrived, the helping neighbours made their exits through a side door. Tuma's mother, however, did not come out: the elderly hostess had prevailed on her to join the feast; explaining, upon the latter's protestations, that she needed extra hands to help carry the food trays to the diners. A large piece of linen was placed at the centre of the sitting room, over the carpet, where the lady guests partook of the feast. The hostess—a plump lady with a wide gentle face and an amicable disposition—joined Tuma's mother who, together with the elderly female escorts of the royal guests, ate their food at the far end of the room. She refused the insistent invitation of the latter to eat with them, saying that she did not want to miss the delicious gossip the elderly maids were certain to disclose about their mistresses. The guests, who were very old themselves, cackled with laughter. They knew that the well-informed hostess was merely observing the traditional courtesy of not joining honoured guests in a meal, lest her presence restrain them from partaking of their fill of the food.

At the completion of their meals the hostess offered Tuma's mother a parcel of food for her daughter, and suggested that she be fetched to collect it. Tuma, wearing her outdoor dress, hung about with the other neighbourhood girls, contenting themselves with the glimpses of affluence within the big house. A little girl came to summon her and Tuma, knowing that her mother was still preoccupied within, was not surprised. She guessed that her mother wanted to send a message to Fatu that she would be delayed. She entered the house through the side door as the lady guests rose to wash their hands out in the open space between the two wings of the house. Her entrance also coincided with the passing of the only male guest in the party, who likewise, came into the open to wash his hands. Tuma diffidently greeted the ladies from a distance. Then she saw the male guest, whom she immediately recogized as the youth who had inquired where she lived when she was at the beach a few weeks back. Their eyes met and the royal visitor, a slight smile showing in his closed lips, nodded gravely as he walked past her with quiet dignity.

The lady of the house took a long time to hand the parcel of food to Tuma. She made small talk, inquiring about her health and whether she went to school. The latter replied quietly and briefly in the affirmative. She felt everyone's gaze directed on her and she became uncomfortable. She took a firm grip of the parcel and then quickly made her exit.

Naza filled a huge silver-plated jug with water and poured it slowly, through its beak-like opening, into the hands of the cleansing guest. The water dripped through the hands and into a receptacle, which was also silver-plated, kept for that purpose. He did the same to Tuma's mother as well as the maids. The hostess then introduced the former to her guests, who praised her cooking and invited her to sit with them. In a conversational manner, they probed at her background with casual inquiries. She responded to their inquires simply and respectfully, but pursed her lips in annoyance when a gaunt lady with poor sight insisted on knowing every detail on her lineage. The scrawny lady, who was also hard of hearing, failed to grasp the substance of the replies Tuma's mother now unenthusiastically supplied. To avoid further aggravating the latter's discomposure with continuous repetitions, a helpful member of the entourage bent her head close to the former and yelled a single word containing the gist of the communication, which she translated into Arabic for ease of understanding. But further queries brought similar spells of incomprehension. Again the woman, who seemed adept at this chore, bent her head close to the interrogator and screeched thunderously a single word from a particularly vague statement, from which the inquisitor was expected to infer the general content. The hostess interposed quickly to say that her neighbour had a claim to nothing short of the best Arab blood. She stated the name of the clan to which the woman's late grandfather had belonged.

A week later Tuma's mother was called to the big house and a message was delivered to her to the effect that Mirza—the young man who had come for lunch—insisted, despite some reservations on the part of his parents, to propose marriage to Tuma provided the girl and her parents were agreeable. Tuma's mother was flustered by the unexpected news. The other lady, noting this, stressed that she could take her time to consider the matter as a formal proposal would be forwarded only after she relayed a firm acquiescence from her and her daughter.

Tuma heard the news from her aunt Fatu. She was not particularly surprised, although the idea stirred her imagination somewhat. She had never entertained thoughts of riches or grandeur, nor could she make out any difference between the marriage of Mwada and that of a princess.

It was then that she tried to explain to her aunt the undefined panic she felt whenever she was approached by a man. Fatu in turn told her sister what Tuma had said. The older woman cackled with amusement. "You will grow up", she reassured her daughter. "It happens to all the little ones". Fearing that her untutored daughter would scandalize the famed family, the woman did not send word of consent on the proposal for Tuma's matrimony; and the royal house did not pursue the matter further.

Tuma waited to grow up. She waited for the vague fear of men to clarify so she would understand things that other girls her age understood, and which they seemed to take for granted. Often she felt that she was on the verge of comprehension. But the enlightment would slip out of her conscious reach just as she was about to grasp it. The mystery came close to revelation one night as she was returning from the seashore, together with a fattish companion, and two men followed behind. Tuma was afraid, but her companion reassured her, saying that she knew the men and that they lived near her home. The fat girl directed Tuma to a place far from their neighbourhood. They walked through several backyards before they arrived at a house the fat girl had said belonged to her uncle. The place was dark and deserted, and the door to the room was closed. Tuma was charged with apprehension, but she also felt a thrill of anticipation. The two men who had followed them approached in the dark and, after a whispered conference with the fat girl, came into view. One of them produced a key from his pocket and struggled with the door-lock. After prolonged efforts the lock opened and the men walked into the room. The women followed.

It was dark inside. One of the men lit a match-stick and fetched a lamp, but the flame kept going out. The fat girl giggled. The man shook the lamp in disgust to gauge the fuel. He tried again. The flame held and gave a shady luminosity that barely enabled them to see each other. With a start Tuma recognized one of the men, and Naza smiled at her.

The other man, who was much taller than Naza, very black and unhandsome, pulled the fat girl to one corner of the small chamber. Naza and Tuma sat on the small bed which gave off a strong odour of sweaty uncleanliness. Naza, his face earnest, started to talk. He told Tuma that he knew of the proposal his mother had relayed to them. He went on to tell her than his parents were keen to see her married away as they were greatly disturbed by his pronounced interest in her, fearing that it would distract him from his studies. His parents, he revealed, wanted him to travel abroad to further his studies.

Tuma listened with thrilled interest but little understanding. She gazed at him in wide-eyed wonderment. She did not know that she mattered sufficiently to be a distress to the notable and the wealthy, nor that she could be the cause of his distraction from his studies. She wanted to say something, but she didn't know what. She giggled.

Fussy noises issued from a corner. Tuma was embarrassed. Naza grinned. Slowly he reached his hand to her and caressed her bosom. Tuma kept still. The boy's advances progressed until his breathing became irregular. Then he sat up and pushed Tuma urgently under him. She yielded. But as he fussed with her underclothes, trying to pull them off, she felt sudden panic. She pushed him away and wriggled out of reach. The youth, now highly aroused, grasped for her. Tuma resisted and got out of bed. A short struggle ensued and Naza slapped her face viciously. The blow missed her; only his fingers made impact. She had not felt any pain, but she felt other, stronger emotions she could not determine. She screamed. It was the shock from the strange emotions, rather than any sensation of hurt, that had made her scream. The man in the corner rose to his feet, cursing. He hissed at them to be quiet and warned them in a muffled whisper that there were people in an adjoining room. Naza buttoned his slacks. Tuma walked out of the room.

Before falling asleep that night, Tuma wondered why she had screamed: she knew that she hadn't felt any pain. She woke up abruptly early in the morning feeling powerful erotic urges. The pressure increased in tempo and urgency until her body was rigid with desire. She writhed and raised her rear up over the mattress. Fatu, who slept in the only bed in the room, stirred from sleep. She inquired sleepily whether there was anything the matter. Tuma groaned and said that nothing was wrong. Fatu sat up, hugged her knees with her hands and gazed at her niece. It was just before sunrise and the room was bathed in the glow of the approaching dawn. Fatu giggled. She got out of bed and giggled some more as she walked past her niece to the door. The latter rose with difficulty and threw herself onto the bed. There was no let úp in her orgy of sexual demands. She used her fingers to manipulate herself, her torso moving up and down fretfully. But release would not come. She got out of bed, walked to the backyard and poured some hot water Fatu had boiled into a bucket, and went to the toilet. She added cold water into the bucket to obtain temperate warmth and then, using her hand, splased the water into her genitals. But this manner of plodding release proved unsatisfactory, too. She returned to bed and again used her fingers to induce sexual release. Finally, after numerous false starts, she reached orgasm. It was an unimpassioned orgasm that caused her anal canal to ache with the strain. The satisfaction was less due to erotic satiation than to relief from pressure.

18

Fatu left the house and went to live with her relatives in the fields. Sumani, Tuma's father, came more often and frequently slept with the family he had deserted. He wore the same pantalone, which had become a size too large on the waist and had added another fold. It now hung on him lopsidedly. He had grown much older. He spent most of his time with the neighbours and returned in the evenings, when he would perch himself on a jutting of the ground in front of the house and curse at imaginary rascals who, he claimed, had impeded his progress in life in order that he should fall to the same low level as themselves. Sometimes he walked to the marketplace early in the morning and returned at noon with vegetables and some mutton. Tuma fried small fish which her mother sold, in addition to the sweetbeans. Her escapades to the sea-shore became less frequent: her companions had either left the neighbourhood or had gotten married. She spent most of her time cooking and scrubbing the room Fatu had vacated and which now belonged to her. She also mopped the small kitchen and the backyard.

Rapid changes came to pass. Violence broke out in the streets. Opposing factions from a once harmonious community jumped at each other's throat, prodded by political orators. Gangs of lawless avengers broke into the shops, slaughtered the terrified owners and looted their meagre merchandize. Tuma's mother was also killed in the general confusion. Her father, who cursed the agitators and called them names, was taken to prison. Naza's home was also broken into. The family, however, managed to escape to the fields where they joined a faction of resisters sympathetic to their cause. Tuma escaped to the neighbours. She slept in an enclosed yard with several other women, most of whom had also escaped from their homes. A few days later, a man came to fetch her. He introduced himself as her cousin and said that Fatu had sent for her. Together they walked to the town-centre and waited for the bus to take them to the country-side. After a day-long wait they found transportation and headed for the village. She stayed with her aunt and helped her to pick fruit and collect vegetables which they carried to the market-place. One day a man came to look for her: he had a letter from her father. The man directed her to deliver the letter to a shop-owner who lived in the next village. He explained that the letter and the directives came from Sumani who was in prison. The woman walked to the village and duly delivered the letter. The shop-owner was a small man with an enormous beard. He accepted the proffered envelope without enthusiasm. He opened it and retrieved the letter. He then placed the sheet of paper on his knee and, using both his hands, pulled it from one side to the other to straighten the folds. At last he held the letter close to his eyes and took in the contents with industrious concentration. He read a few lines and then raised his head to peer at the women. He bent over it again and digested the balance of the message. Finally he folded the letter and replaced it into the envelope. He looked at Tuma with sharp concentration and a shadow of a smile creased the sides of his lips. But immediately the smile faded and his eyes dulled with exhausted patience. "I told him not to run from place to place", he commented. He pointed his finger to the door which led into the shanty.

Tuma stayed in the old man's house. Fatu returned to the fields. The old man, who she discovered was her paternal uncle, had a large family consisting of two wives and some dozen children of various ages. The women were less than enthusiastic at Tuma's arrival, but they tolerated her presence when they learned that she was a relative of their husband and not another competitor in the bulging household. The old man was given to absent-mindedness and occasional bouts of moodiness.

Often he ignored Tuma. At other times he looked askance at her, as though he was surprised at her presence in the house. At still other times he talked to her cheerfully. Once, as he was preparing himself for his noon prayers, he noticed her. She was helping his elder wife with the house cleaning. He was in a jovial mood. "I told your father not to run from place to place", he said cheerfully. He waved his bony hands to exhibit his possessions, which included his wives and the toddlers. "Look at me", he went on, "I don't own much, but I am settled down, thank God. Now it is he who is asking me to take care of his child".

Abruptly, the jovial mood passed. "I told him not to run from place to place", he concluded as he bent to wash his feet.

Preparations were underway for the whole family to travel to Arabia. Tuma learned that she was also included in the plans. Word always came from the town that arrangements for their travel were completed and a date was set for the voyage. But as the appointed day neared, they were informed that some hitch had been encountered and the journey was postponed. When, finally, a firm date was set, the family gathered their belongings and moved to the town. Tuma requested permission to collect a few of her belongings from her old home. She found the house much the same except for the air of desolation surrounding it. She entered the house and found Mwada, who appeared to have settled comfortably, with her belongings scattered all over the small backyard. She welcomed Tuma and hugged her affectionately. She explained that she had moved into the house for fear that the new authorities would confiscate it if it was left unattended. She introduced Tuma to a thin, elderly man who sat near a firewood who, she said, was her husband.

Tuma collected her belongings, including some cooking utensils and her mirror—which still hung on the wall—and bade Mwada goodbye.

The family stayed at the town-centre all day long and waited. The women sat on their haunches and talked. The children played about noisily. Night came and they still waited patiently. Then, late at night, a guide appeared and instructed them to follow him. Leaving their luggage behind, as instructed by the guide, they walked the short distance to the harbour, past the iron-works and cranes to the edge of the pier and on to a small, overloaded vessel that seemed ill-equipped for the long voyage.

Several days passed before the small ships took to the high seas. More passengers arrived. People moved in and out and noisy preparations were made. When word was finally given that the voyage would start the following morning, Tuma's uncle came to bid his family good-bye. She went down to thank him and to bid him farewell. The old man looked at her in surprise at first, but immediately his face glowed with intelligence.

"You are ---Tuma", he exclaimed with a cheerful smile. Tuma proffered her hand, but the old man appeared not to notice it. Abruptly his smile faded and his expression became vacant. "I told him not to run from place to place". He stressed as he turned and went his way.

After weeks of a sea-tossed voyage, Tuma and her newly-acquired family arrived at the Gulf of Oman. There were several days of delay before Government formalities were completed and they were allowed to disembark. Tuma, as with all her fellow migrants, struggled to adapt herself as best she could to the new environment. Her cousins worked hard and earned enough to provide their family with necessities and, progressively, a measure of comfort. She also worked, running errands and selling vegetables at the roadside. She managed to provide herself with her own room fitted with an air conditioning unit. She purchased a bed and hung her mirror near it. Basic structural changes gradually transformed the environment. Modest constructions mushroomed and turned the dry landscape into a beehive of industry. The bustle of activity brought ever-increasing rewards to Tuma and her benefactors. She bought new clothes and added furniture to her room.

With some leisure and a measure of comfort, thoughts other than those of mere survival awakened in her. She thought of marriage, and the rewards from a harmonious relationship far greater than those Mwada or her aunt Fatu had ever known. For she had glimpsed at lifestyles qualitatively different, had felt the thrills from surmounted hardships and the simple joys from the returns of hard toil.

Halim was a soft-spoken, likeable young man who lived a short distance from Tuma's home. Every morning, as he walked to the office, he saw Tuma. He smiled and curtsied to her. On his return from work he would stop to chat with her. Tuma encouraged him to develop the acquaintanceship. She liked him and she was attracted by his innocence and gentle bearing Halim was everybody's favourite, and the topic of daily conversations. Everyone talked of his diligence in his work and the high sense of moral responsibility he had toward his kin. The only grown-up male in the family, he supported his mother, several young relatives and numerous dependents, all of whom lived under one roof and looked to him for their feed. Tuma was flattered by the attention of one so manly and popular. Unconsciously, she wondered that she did not feel panic when he drew near her. She was reassured by the feeling that she had out grown her childhood drawback. At night Tuma thought of Halim. She imagined how it would feel like to yield to his gentle embrace, and she felt a tingling sensation below her tummy. Someday soon, she thought, she would have to surrender herself to a man's embrace. She had to grow up sometime, she told herself. She smiled indulgently at the idea. She opened her mouth and teased herself childishly with her tongue.

Occasionally, neighbours came to visit. They gossiped about other neighbours and talked of their new household purchases. Recently, the gossip was focussed on property acquisitions. The women talked of the houses their sons had promised to build for them. They described the type of furniture they would buy and the decor they would put on their new homes. It was during one of these visits that a pleasant, elderly lady who seemed to take a great liking for Tuma inquired about the latter's life prior to her journey to the new land. Tuma told of her mother who was killed in the uprising and of her father who was imprisoned. The lady then asked Tuma whether she had any grandchildren.

Tuma's eyes widened. She looked at her elderly visitors with innocent incomprehension. She rose and, in a dream-like stance, walked to her bedroom, her eyes reflecting disbelief. Panic gripped her. She knew what she would see on the mirror—she had always seen it—but her instincts fought against the obvious.

She looked at her reflection on the mirror, and saw what she had always seen—with the basic difference that this time she understood what she saw. Of course she was no longer the prettiest girl in the land. She was a very old woman.

The screen that had shuttered her mind from understanding lifted suddenly. In an instant she understood everything she had failed to grasp through the years: she understood now the feeling she always had of wanting to do something she didn't know what it was, and then found herself looking at her mirror: a part of her mind was warning her that time was passing. She understood then why she had screamed when Naza slapped her: the profoundly pleasurable sensation of the pressure of his fingers on her flesh had made her scream. It was the excess of pleasure that had brought about the mysterious sensation that had thrown her into a panic. She understood now the subsequent agony of sexual desires she couldn't satisfy. She now realized that she had denied herself that which she desired the most: the love of a man.

She had been tricked out of a life-time of supreme, and certain bliss.

She had been denied even simple sex; a commodity so plentiful that her aunt Fatu had been bored with it she tolerated a man's embrace only when she needed a new pair of shoes. She could have been married to the wealthy and the noble. Instead, she had waited to grow up—and had waited half a life-time too long.

A pressure of her hand, and a slap on her face were the two occurrences in her life which had given her pleasure. These in addition to hard toil and perseverance in her old age. But the loss of a life-time, and the regrets of how it might have been could be withstood.

It was the pain that could not be absorbed. When the matured, firmly—rooted misconception gorged itself off her head, it pulverized her mind and carried with it a lot of her emotions—as a strong tree, forcibly uprooted, carried plenty of earth within it's orb. Rather than accomodate such gross irrationality, her reason revolted. Her mind fell apart, her faculties disintegrated.

Of course Hamid displayed innocent interest in her: she was old enough to be his grandmother.

Tuma wanted to scream. Instead, she laughed hysterically.

And thence, day in and day out, the old woman shrieked hysterically every so often. It was a hauntingly distressing sound: half tormented, half humorous.

I recalled the face of the affable woman at the clinic. To have suspected that within that calm, serene disposition there lay hidden an avalanche of volcanic eruptions, of once firm, if simple, beliefs. And what, after all (and this was a question she must have asked herself many times) had she done to deserve the meting out of justice of such magnitude of vengeful fury? Her crime was the failure to grasp the truth ly uncovered its face.

Tuma believed she was tied to the ground because her simple mind was naturally susceptible to such beliefs. She remained that way until sheer weariness had forced her to raise her head. The realisation that there never was any rope around her neck in the first place made her mad. What power had the right to tie someone's neck with an illusory chain, until near the end of her days, and then proc' her to unchain herself.

Her shrieks attracted but a glance from a flustered pedestrian. Her people nagged her to go to the hospital for treatment. They couldn't know that there was neither treatment nor relief for her condition: her memory would always remain with her. The cauldron of flaming emotions inside her head could not be extinguished. The mutiny of her sensibilities could not be disciplined. Only time could stabilize the chaos, and there wasn't much of that. She could not understand that the whole world did not perceive the torment she was in. No one would believe it if she were able to describe it to them.

The most she had desired from life was meagre indeed. That Fate should have cheated her out of so little was incomprehensible. That she should have suffered so formidable a degree of anguish as punishment for wasting her life was mind-boggling. Few would believe that such a mishap could occur. Fewer still could possibly understand the painful effect.

A clanking noise interrupted my reverie. It was time for supper. I got off the blanket-covered floor and picked my tin plate and cup.

'I did', I thought, completing my reverie as I handed my dinner plate, and noted with pleasure that it was a Monday and there was a welcome change of diet.

'Oh yes. I understood.'